MW01065094

Rediscover the Apron
Satisfying Spiritual Starvation

Tammy Lovell Stone

Rediscover the Apron: Satisfying Spiritual Starvation
By Tammy Lovell Stone

Editor-in-Chief: Loral Robben Pepoon
Critique Team: Judith Drake, Susan Music and Glenda Lovell

Cover Design: Jennifer Smith
Cover Photo: Tammy Lovell Stone

All Scripture quotations, unless otherwise indicated, are taken from the HOLY BIBLE, THE NEW KING JAMES VERSION Copyright © 1992 by Thomas Nelson, Inc. Used by permission. All rights reserved.

THE HOLY BIBLE, NEW INTERNATIONAL VERSION®, NIV® Copyright © 1973, 1978, 1984, 2011 by Biblica, Inc.™ Used by permission. All rights reserved worldwide.

Scripture quotations marked KJV are taken from the *King James Version* of the Bible.

The true events in this book are told from the authors perspective and from the authors memory of them. To protect individual privacy the author may have in some instances changed names, locations, and/or circumstances.

ISBN-13: 978-0692520789 (Tammy Lovell Stone)
ISBN-10: 0692520783

Printed in the United States of America

Notice of Rights
All rights reserved. No part of this book may be reproduced or transmitted in any form by any means, electronic, mechanical, photocopy, recording or other without the prior written permission of the publisher.

For information on getting permission for reprints and excerpts, contact: Tammylovellstone.com.

Author Website: Tammylovellstone.com

Editor Website: cowriterpro.com

Copyright © 2015 Tammy Lovell Stone

Dedication

I dedicate this book to my God and Heavenly Father who taught me a new way, a better way. Thank you for never giving up on your children. Your love and forgiveness have transformed my world and allowed me to share this journey with others.

Terri,

I pray you are encouraged as you read this book. May God draw you closer to Him as you follow His plan for your life.

Sammy

Contents

Acknowledgements

God has blessed me and guided me as I embarked on the journey of writing this book. He gave me encouragement and provision to persevere, even when it seemed that there was no way. But, God makes His own way. He is not bound by finances, intellectual hindrances or fear.

I want to thank everyone, even strangers, who listened intently as I told them about many of the principles God was pouring into me. They were His words. They still are. I will never forget the friendships that were forged. Thank you to my friends and family who read the early versions of this book and cheered me on.

Hats off to Heartprint Writers Group for your constant support and accountability in helping me to arrive where I am today. Thanks to Loral Robben Pepoon: You are more than just an editor, you are a gift from God. Your guidance and skill in helping me expound on what God implanted in my heart is still an amazement to me.

I appreciate my sisters in Christ, Judith Drake and Susan Music, who humble me with their generosity, especially by giving the time necessary to proofread this book. Your loving nudges kept me on the right track and you both were a big part of my cheering squad pushing me over the finish line on this project. Job well done, ladies!

Thank you Jennifer Smith for your excellent work on the cover design and your determination in helping me meet my deadline. Shannon and Missy Stone: You are a true brother and sister in Christ. Thanks for sponsoring the cover design. Thanks so much to Naturally You Market which agreed to host my first book signing. A special shout goes out to my friend, Jeanie Bishop, who lent me her camera to take the cover photo. You are a sweetheart!

To my mother, Glenda Lovell, who has loved me unconditionally my entire life and never let me doubt that I could do anything I put my mind to. You taught me the most important lesson of my life in showing me that persevering in faith and trust in Jesus Christ is the only way to live. To my husband, Kenny, who gave me the freedom to pursue what God placed on my heart: You are and forever will be my soul mate. You complete me perfectly. To my children Ashton, Charley and Gabe: Thanks for eating microwave meals, suffering through days when your mother was either behind closed doors or distracted by a flood of thoughts bouncing around in her head. And to Britt and Boone, my grandchildren: Mum can come out to play now.

Introduction

Little children, let no one deceive you. He who practices righteousness is righteous, just as He is righteous.
1 John 3:7, NKJV

Part 1: My Story

I don't want life to drive me. I want God to guide me. It is 2 a.m. and I awaken as if from a nightmare. I am covered in sweat. My heart is racing and my pulse is quick. I am breathing as if I have just run a marathon. I jump out of bed and begin to pace the floor. The house is quiet but my spirit is not. My body is shaking and I can't seem to calm down. I rush to the emergency room because I could not regain my composure, nor could I catch my breath. My heart seemed to be racing even though I couldn't figure out why. As I wait to see the doctor, I have no doubt that I will receive the most dreadful news.

After what seemed like an eternity of testing and checking my vital signs the physician says, "You are having a panic attack." Who me, Mrs. "Reserved Under Pressure" and "Calm as a Cucumber?" I was devastated. At that moment, with the diagnosis and my family history of mental illness looming in my mind, I completely shut down.

Because I was emotionally incapacitated, I would spend the next week in bed unable to handle even the sweet voices of my children. They couldn't understand why their normally nurturing mommy wouldn't talk or cuddle with them. I could not express anything I was feeling. I was simply exhausted and unable to get out of bed. My parents came to stay with me during the day and our children were shipped off to other family members. I was put on medication and my outgoing personality and self-confidence left me.

How did I get to this place, being unable to function? I had such hopes and dreams. I was a good person. I had always obeyed the law, and

I was kind and hard working. Because of my family history of mental illness, people might leap to the conclusion that genetics may have played a role. But, they would be wrong. I had been dangling at the end of my rope for quite some time. I had just finally let go and fallen into the pit of despair. I was here because I had chosen to live without God's continual guidance and influence in my life.

I had asked Him to live in my heart at the age of 12. I had accepted His invitation to live in Heaven, but I had absolved myself of the responsibility and accountability that come with citizenship in God's Kingdom. He is the King. He makes the rules. He even gives us the rulebook (the Bible), which leaves us without an excuse to claim lack of knowledge about Him or about how His Kingdom operates.

I had failed to read this rulebook. I did not truly know God's character. I lived the way I saw fit. I said I would be His when I accepted His Son, Jesus. However, I wasn't living life by His rules. I believed my life was my own; by all appearances, I was living an upstanding life. I was faithful in my marriage and I was a mother concerned about the welfare of her children. I didn't steal or cheat. I never even drank or smoked. But I was a lukewarm Christian. I rarely attended church. I prayed only when I needed help from God, and I hardly ever studied the Bible. I didn't see the need. I didn't understand its importance.

The Bible, however, is clear about how God feels about the person I used to be. Revelation 3:16 paints a vivid picture of God's distaste for the lukewarm. He says that He will vomit us out of His mouth. That doesn't sound too good, does it! I am thankful that God's love is so much greater than his displeasure in my behavior. Because of His great love for me, God did what any loving parent would when their child's life is headed in the wrong direction—He staged an intervention. His intervention was my bout with panic attacks.

During that season of anxiety, I knew I needed help and I went to see a counselor. The room where I met with a counselor for the first time was quiet and subtly lit. A labrador retriever was laying on the rug in front of a short couch. On that day, I only remember one topic of discussion: I had asked her to teach me how to overcome my panic disorder without medication.

I was opposed to using medication because I have always had a sensitivity to synthetic ingredients in food and medication. In my experience, dealing with illness by natural means is usually easier than dealing with the side effects of chemicals. I had also heard that anti-depressants and anti-anxiety medication can leave the mind numb. My father was an alcoholic, and I watched as he used vodka to numb his pain from issues that seemed to overwhelm him. I feared that I might become dependent on anti-depressant and anti-anxiety drugs in very much the same way. I had seen that struggle and wanted no part of it. I also did not want to use medication as a crutch. I wanted complete healing, not just an easing of my symptoms.

The counselor believed healing without the medication was possible in my case because I was the type of person that could examine my life with intentionality, and then do the work to make the necessary changes. I was going to have to fight to regain my freedom from my struggles and fear. I was going to have to muster the will to fight with all my strength because I knew no one had time to babysit a woman who couldn't get on the interstate, drive to an unknown destination or take a short ride in an elevator without hyperventilating. Over time, I would have to do my part to be victorious in the fight. Then, my counselor would never have to see me again.

Her words about no longer needing to see me would prove to be true. I did do the hard work myself, with God at the center of the fight. I remained under my counselor's guidance, and I took an anti-depressant for about six months. I followed her advice, which included setting aside time for myself and processing negative emotions more productively and realistically. These strategies helped me recover and taught me how to prevent future panic attacks.

Before my season of anxiety attacks, I had always been strong, healthy, smart and dedicated to whatever task was in front of me. Every time I experienced failure, personal loss or anything else that was exceedingly difficult, I would put my game face on and act as if nothing were wrong. I had practiced this skill for so long that I was successful appearing as if I had it all together. My feelings on the inside, however, were warning me something was not right. I would ignore the warnings, and tell myself to suck it up and deal with my hurt later. But later would come, and I still wouldn't take the time I needed to deal with my hurt. You see, after the crisis passed, I saw no reason to dwell on it. I never gave myself time to adjust to the loss, disappointment or conflict within personal relationships. With the regular demands of life, I guess I never felt I had the time.

Looking back at this time before the panic attacks, I realize my hidden feelings weren't just my internal warnings that I could put off, but they were also God's warning signs that something needed to change. After the panic attacks occurred, however, I wanted to get to the center of my issue and resolve it at the source instead of covering it up. I had put on a mask too many times and the result was overflowing anxiety. I knew it was time to unearth the root.

The root of my problem was deception and it was fed by an age-old misconception. I had been taught that any good upstanding Southern woman should live to please her husband. After all, the woman described in Proverbs 31 is trusted by her husband and works hard for her household. I was deceived because I had bought into the idea that all spouse pleasing was godly marital service. I had—without realizing it—placed my husband in the position where my Father God belonged.

Maybe my behavior was part of the curse mentioned in Genesis 3:16. Like all women after Eve, my desire would be for my man. But, I was blinded to the reality that my devotion to my husband was misplaced. God's Truth was distorted because I did not compare my understanding of a marital relationship to the beautifully redeemed biblical relationship between a husband and a wife living with Christ at the center of their lives. To understand what that restored relationship looks like, I would need to first understand the relationship I needed with God as an individual. I would need a more focused relationship with God if I was going to overcome the anxiety-stricken state I was in. I needed to understand that God's love was enough—even when my husband's actions seemed to say, "I don't cherish you."

Cherishing encompasses caring about the welfare of a person in a way that says, "I am willing to sacrifice my wants so that your emotional, physical and spiritual needs are met." The opposite of being cherished is insisting on having everything go according to your plan, even if it crushes or suffocates the will of another. My husband, although he loved me, didn't understand that his behavior was not cherishing me. He wanted everything to be done according to his specifications, including laundry, dishes and other housework that he thought should be finished by the time he arrived home each day. No matter what was accomplished, he always found at least one task to complain about. His frustration with my inability to meet his demands only solidified my misunderstanding that I only needed to try harder. This situation and my mindset caused anxiety to rise every time I heard his truck pull into the driveway.

Devoting my life to my family didn't feel like the wrong thing to do at the time—nor is it really now. But if my devotion to my family is put above my devotion to God, then my family has become an idol. We are to have no other gods before Him.[1] Anything we spend our time, money and energy on more than God is an idol.

[1] Exodus 20:3

When we live to please another more than God, we are giving that person power over us in a way we might not realize. Our happiness becomes directly related to how pleased that person is with us at any given time. In my case, the more I worked to please my husband, the less pleased he seemed to be. He was only reacting to the impossibly high position I had given him in my life—it was as if I had allowed my husband to become my god. Usually human gods are very disagreeable when they don't get what they want. My husband was no exception. I could no longer please him because I felt defeated. I was defeated because I could no longer please him. My husband did not have the power to redeem me from this brokenness. Only God could do that. I had not yet opened my heart enough to allow God to be in His proper position (at the center of my life) so that He could heal me.

I struggled for twenty years because I would not open God's Word and allow His truths to heal me. My mind was bankrupt because I had been making withdrawals emotionally that entire time without adding enough nurturing deposits. I stayed trapped because I had created a mold for myself based on all I believed and did. I claimed to be a Christian, but I didn't think it was important to live for God. I felt Bible study and church attendance was optional and unnecessary for living as a Christian. I skipped church for months at a time, rarely praying or reading the Bible. I treated prayer as a wish list and a get out of jail free card instead of spending my time building a relationship between me and my Father God. My distorted view of Christianity left me not knowing that I was living contrary to God's teachings. I misunderstood who I was to God and what He should mean to me. In short, I allowed myself to become spiritually starved.

The lessons I learned about God, the truth I learned about a healthy marital relationship and about expressing myself helped build the foundation that enables me to thrive today. This knowledge was not really a result of counseling, although counseling for a season was beneficial. The wisdom I gained was a result of my God-given desire to seek Him and live for Him regardless of the consequences. I was brought back to God because I learned to trust Him through difficult situations that left me nowhere to turn but to Him. I learned that church was a much needed life-support system and a venue for living out my service to God. I discovered that Bible study keeps me from being deceived by ideas that don't agree with what God says. When I am walking with God and alert, I am able to recognize deception. Through this alertness, I am also able to overcome ensnaring temptations that could lure me on a detour and result in shame and destruction.

God worked in my life in such a way that I could not keep His work or His message contained. I still can't keep quiet about what He has done! The relationships in my life now are so much better than they were that night I arrived in the emergency room. My husband and I have a strong marital relationship with the proper boundaries. Those boundaries include our devotion to God as individuals and our love for each other as a couple. My husband submits to God's authority, and I have the freedom to live 100% sold out for Jesus. I submit to God's authority and can be the helper that my husband needs, even if that means telling him something that will not please him. I can be a wife who wants him to achieve all that God has planned for him.

Because of both my deliverance from anxiety and my husband's transformation, I now have the courage to live abundantly. God has done immeasurably and abundantly more than I could have ever asked for. I want to continue to live life God's way, which leads to peace and fearless abandonment. I gave up control of my life and tying my joy to my circumstances and earthly relationships. I know that God is pleased with my devotion to Him, even though I sometimes fail and have shortcomings. Because my life is so much fuller and vibrant than before, I want to share the lessons God taught me about Himself and my relationship with Him.

My hope is that you also may be encouraged in your time of need. I pray you come to the realization that God is trustworthy and He alone is the One who draws us from where we are. No matter how far away we may be, He brings us unto Himself. He wants to be involved in our everyday lives. He wants us to walk with Him instead of just knowing about Him. We are His beloved children. He wants to spend each day with us until He calls us home forever.

Part 2: This Book

I still remember the day in 2005 when God gave me the title for this book. I was standing in my kitchen pondering the reason aprons were no longer a staple in the American female wardrobe. In the 1950s, every mother and grandmother seemed to have one—they might have many, in fact. Maybe some feel—like I did—that aprons are just a little too old fashioned. At that time, I had recently "rediscovered" the apron's main purpose: to protect the clothing underneath. It wasn't old fashioned. It was practical; and I'm all about practical.

Eight years passed from the time God gave me the title of this book before I would look to see what the Bible has to say about the word apron. The Book of Acts says, "And God wrought special miracles by the hands of Paul: So that from his body were brought unto the sick handkerchiefs or aprons, and the diseases departed from them, and the evil spirits went out of them" (Acts 19:11–12, KJV). As I searched, I began to see how God had freed me from my anxiety-stricken season in many respects by giving me a desire to study His Word more deeply. God also eventually showed me that His teachings in Scripture have an ability to protect us in very much the same way as an apron protects us. His Apron of protection shields us from unnecessary heartache or enslavement. For me, tying on His Apron strings has protected me from slipping into my old familiar sins of self-sufficiency, people pleasing, materialism and greed. His Apron has healed me by giving me a peace, a healthy fear of God and a deep trust in Almighty God who provides everything I need emotionally, financially and spiritually.

The journey that God launched in me that day in the emergency room has led to freedom from the shackles I put into place to restrict my biblical diet. The person God created me to be could not blossom until I received the proper nourishment from my Heavenly Father. The nourishment He has placed in my life—and that he has given to all His children—is found in the Bible.

I am inviting you on a journey with me as you read *Rediscover the Apron*. My prayer is that you will see how Jesus invites us into the kitchen to His table to rediscover His dinner feast. After he lovingly lavishes us with an exquisite meal, He equips us, giving us His Apron. He sharpens our spiritual senses as we become aware of the voice of God. He gives us focus to see Him through the distractions. As we see Him more clearly, we will know Jesus better so we don't have a case of mistaken identity when the adversary, Satan, tries to pose as light. Jesus will also give us a deeper sense of understanding our own identity in Him. As our eyes are set on Him, He helps us run the race He has set before us. As we excel in our relay, we will learn to trust Him even more deeply. Through that process, he will foster stronger compassion in us for others. We will gain a greater depth of freedom when we take a break from activity and make ourselves still. We will find that He will help us die to ourselves. We will have a reality check as we seek Him to cultivate our heart toward repentance. And, finally, we will have a God-given motivation to conquer whatever difficulty is before us, claiming victory over our circumstances. This victory, along with the many blessings He will bestow on us, will help us give others the courage to do the same.

Are you up for the challenge? Get your aprons ready, and be sure that you tie the strings tightly.

Chapter 1
Dinner

Blessed are those who hunger and thirst for righteousness, For they shall be filled.
Matthew 5:6, NKJV

An empty white plate is set before me. It brightens the dark mahogany of the banquet size table where I find myself. Illuminating the table's center is a light. It penetrates the darkness that keeps me from clearly seeing all the characteristics of the room. The light's warmth causes me to close my eyes and bask in its soul calming glow.

I remain silent as appetizers and entrees are passed toward me. The food is down home Southern cooking: piping hot cornbread from a cast iron skillet, chicken fried crispy like grandma used to make, real mashed potatoes smothered with sawmill gravy, buttermilk biscuits still steaming from the oven, fresh butter churned this morning and honey glazed ham with pineapples on top. Fresh tomatoes from the garden along with green beans and fried okra are soon added. Because it's a hot summer's day, I have the option of washing these delicacies down with a nice glass of sweet tea or perhaps some fresh squeezed lemonade. I can choose to top off this fantastic feast with delicious desserts including: pecan pie, peach cobbler, coconut or angel food cake served with fresh strawberries and ice cold watermelon. I could even have a piece of shoe fly pie. The bounty is unbelievable, like nothing I have ever seen. Each item is prepared to perfection and my desire for just a taste of it all is piqued.

In anticipation, I wait for what seems like a very long time wondering why, with the smorgasbord available, does my plate remain clean? It is empty because I haven't filled it. To fill my plate would take action on my part. I would need to physically receive what has been prepared. I almost reach out to help myself to some of the Southern fixins, but my thoughts interrupt me, "What if you don't like the taste of that?" My hand then withdraws leaving my plate vacant. I perceive the abundance yet choose poverty. What would cause me to willingly choose emptiness? How about fear and laziness? Perhaps. A sense of unworthiness? Maybe. Put yourself in this situation. Ask yourself: *Why don't I choose the feast God has for me?*

The banquet before us is God's Word and the plate represents his blessing in our lives. If we are not feeding on the information contained in the Bible, then we are trudging through life unsatisfied—and eventually we will be empty. The life source—along with all the nutrients we will ever need—is passed around the table where we sit, and we say, "No, I don't think so, that's not for me." For a Christian, letting the feast that God has prepared go by should never happen.

Let's sit down to dinner with an old friend, the Ancient of Days, to see what He has for us. Maybe for you, He is a new friend. In either case, let's commune with each other on a higher level—one we may never have experienced before. Let's soak in His countenance and hang on to His every Word, until we leave the table more full than when we arrived. We will leave with a plateful of wisdom and a piece of humble pie. We will be filled with love beyond understanding. Our attitude will be in check, and we will be able to go forth to conquer the hunger and weaknesses in our lives.

Just like our physical diet affects our health, our spiritual diet affects our relationship with God. And, our spiritual diet is no less important than our physical diet. In fact, I feel that our spiritual diet is even more important. But, many people don't really take their spiritual diet seriously. I know before my bout with anxiety, I didn't pay attention to my spiritual food intake. Maybe you are like some who think, "It's all good, God and I have it all worked out." If those are your thoughts, you are deceiving yourself. Unfortunately, you don't really have it all worked out. Your life and your plan could come crashing down at any moment. But, God already has everything worked out for his followers. He has a plan to give you a hope and a future, no matter what your circumstances are.[2]

So, check yourself. If you haven't been hearing from God—or feeding yourself spiritually—it's time to get real and have an intentional spiritual checkup. He requires that His people walk in obedience to His Word. Are you one of His children? Are you walking in obedience? If not, you may be heading for an unrequested wakeup call just like I was.

If we claim Christianity, we have no excuse for spiritual starvation. In the South—the Bible Belt to be exact—where I was born and raised,

---

[2] Jeremiah 29:11

it has been my experience that many are spiritually anorexic from a lack of daily biblical nutrition. Few seem willing to admit their deep hunger. Many live in a sad sort of denial that leads them to believe something like, "I am good because I know God exists. My belief about Him defines who He is and validates my choices." Possessing this attitude is like having the well of life-giving water around every corner but never drinking it. Living with this mindset is also akin to never feeling the refreshment of a spirit-reviving pool. And so, even with a fountain of living water available to us, we walk around thirsty, in a field of dead man's bones with our religious appearance and confidence in what we think we know. I know—because I walked around like that prior to my anxiety attacks and God's intervention in my life. The truth is, however, without feasting on God and His Truth, we are no closer to God than the man who refuses to claim Him at all. As one evangelist I heard recently says, "We are near Jesus, but we do not know Him." Or, "We are connected to Jesus, but we are not consumed with Jesus."

God is so much a part of the Southern culture that we have taken him for granted. We say, "Thank God," without allowing those words to register in our brains or enabling the necessary sentiment of gratitude to form in our hearts. Many of our everyday comments that reference God are said with whimsical thoughtlessness. We seem to have grown lazy in our dedication and devotion to God. Our service to Him has somehow become optional.

As a result of a casual familiarity with God and perhaps not enough reverence, we have become comfortable with sin in our lives. Sins such as hatred, unforgiveness, selfishness, bitterness, or other rancid feelings may find their way into our lives. Many people have an attitude that says, "I can participate in any activity I want as long as it is legal." Living within the confines of the laws of any country is not the same as godly behavior under the guidance of the Holy Spirit. We are called to be holy because God is holy.[3] The relationship we form with our sins causes us to become less aware of our departure from God's plan. Unrepentant sin leads to misery of the soul. This continued pattern of unrepentant sin wears on us like a weight that reduces our energy and effectiveness a little more each day. We can continue down this road of misery and marginal living, or we can get serious and intentional about where we place God in our lives. If we feast on God and His Word, and we eat all the nutrients available to us through church, individual Bible study, small groups and

---

[3] 1 Peter 1:16

regular worship, we will gain strength in Christ so that we can be effective for whatever He calls us to do.

Jesus makes a way for our relationship with God the Father,[4] but God Himself also protects us from the waves of life.[5] If it were not for God's protection—His Apron—a slow erosion and constant decaying of our spirit would take place. Little by little, we would be too weak to function in a way that glorifies God and spiritually our hearts would grow cold. We would also gradually care less about the plight of others. We could become so focused on our goals and stuff that we want or own, and we could fail to notice our elderly neighbor who can't pay the electric bill or afford necessary medication. We could develop an appetite for sexual pleasure that would enslave us and distort the biblical view of sexual intimacy. We could become angry at fellow brothers or sisters in Christ, and instead of praying for them and bearing with them while they work out their salvation, we could then develop a spiritually cold heart.[6] Instead of forgiving others, we might have errant or judgmental attitudes toward them. If we don't have our Apron strings tightly fastened, we could be prone to spend less and less time caring about the work that God says is important and we could spend more time seeking to selfishly control our own destiny for our own gain.

It isn't difficult to see this selfish epidemic of control played out all over the world as you think about it today. Nations are at war either from outside invaders or they are experiencing treachery from within. If we expect our protection to come from our government, healthcare system or our own intellectual knowledge, we are striving in vain to protect ourselves. Only God's Apron—His Ways—offer the protection we need.

As Christ followers, we shouldn't walk without the light of God's Word to guide us. One of the reasons God created the Bible—the "steak" if you will of His dinner table—is to reveal our false ways of thinking. Unfortunately, we have grown so accustomed to our errant thoughts that we will defend them even if Scripture plainly says they are not true. God's standards are not intended to restrict us or bring hardship to our lives. His intention is to protect us from the bondage and guilt we can find ourselves in when we ignore what the Bible says. Taking a stand against God leads us to choices that separate us from God and His merciful hand.

---

[4] 2 Corinthians 5:21
[5] Psalm 91:1-16
[6] Colossians 3:12-13

The necessity for His Apron, His protection, is never more evident than when we remove it. Without it, we are leaving ourselves open and vulnerable—in essence, we are becoming spiritually starved. It is hard to fight off the enemy when we are too weak to stand. It is almost impossible to navigate the land mines of temptation and worldly thinking in our path without God's shield—His Apron—to protect us. But, if we abide in the shadow of the Almighty, He will forever be our refuge and our strength.[7] We will experience His abundance and His peace. Then, we will feel satisfied just as we do after a good southern meal.

Tying God's Apron Strings Around Your Heart

When was the last time you had a meal with Jesus? Why not have one today? Set the table for Him, get out your Bible, play some worship music softly in the background and grab a journal. As you begin your time with God, pray and ask God to meet you. Then, begin to feast on the Psalms or whatever Bible passage comforts you. Thank Him for who He is as you observe His attributes in the Word. Then, ask Him what spiritual food He is asking you to digest. Ask Him about His plans and purposes for your life. Pray about any concerns that you have. Let your conversation with God flow back and forth, taking time to listen and write. Then, pause, taking a few moments to allow what you have received to take root or be tied around your heart. Finally, share what He tells you with at least one other person.

---

[7] Psalm 91:1

Chapter 2
Discover

The heavens declare the glory of God; And the firmament shows His handiwork.
Psalm 19:1, NKJV

Have you ever taken a trip to your local zoo? My family went on that excursion last fall. My children, like most children, were very excited to see the animals. Their shrills made for a noisy hour-and-a-half trip to the zoo in the big city. Once we got there, they darted here and there, grabbing my arm saying, "Look!" They barely gave me time to see anything before they jerked my arm in another direction. Even amidst all of their excitement, I couldn't help marveling at the creatures God has created. Amazing animals were everywhere. We saw everything from a pink flamingo to a blue frog. During my short stay at the zoo, I noticed something else: A presence of peace and serenity seemed to grip that small piece of earth. I really didn't think about the tranquility I experienced there until the last exhibit. I casually approached the fence. I could see three giraffes; each were a different size. My mind immediately thought Papa giraffe, Mama giraffe and Baby giraffe—you know—like the three bears, only skinnier. And just like Goldilocks, I took a moment to step into their world.

As I watched the giraffes, I was in awe. They were using their long tongues to gather food from far up in the trees. Did you know their tongues are about eighteen inches long? Wow! Not only was that fact fascinating to me, but I marveled that they did not seem bothered by me or any of the other visitors at all. These slender giants just continued to munch. Their bodies were enormous. The tallest giraffe was standing in the far corner of the grounds. He was painted with darker tones than the others. Gracefully, but with distinction, he began to walk toward the rest of his family. I must admit—I was amazed at what he was able to communicate without saying a word. I do not know how tall he was, but I know that I have trees in my yard that appear shorter. His presence was unmistakable; his design most unique and his body most beautiful. His dark amber tones that laid on a bed of ivory brought a contrast of vivid color. His stature alone commanded respect. I could tell—at least for this moment—that he had an air about him. I expected to hear the sound of hooves upon the ground as he traveled. But, sounds never met my ear. As he walked, he was much more like a dancer approaching a climactic moment in a performance. He would command the full attention of your eye until, at last, he stops as if to present himself to his audience. Man would have raised his arms and stood firmly as if to say, "Bravo." Yet, the giraffe wasn't nearly so pompous. I could see pride in his strides, but he wasn't presenting himself. He was simply being who God created him to be.

Man—unlike the giraffe who is satisfied just to be—strives to create. Many architectural designs are grand, but I am afraid any man-made structures fail in comparison to the grandeur of this planet. It seems that anyone who does not believe in creation might have a difficult time truly connecting with our natural environment as God intended. Just as He created Eden for Adam and Eve, he has created the Earth and everything in it, for us to enjoy.

When was the last time we slowed down enough to observe and rediscover the uniqueness of anything God has made, including our children. If you are a busy mom like me, it may have been quite a while. Try seeing the world through the eyes of a child, and I think you will see that children view the world differently than we do. They are enthralled with all the cool things that there are to touch and see. For example, little boys can rarely pass an earthworm without picking it up and showing the nearest person. My children are in awe at how things grow in the garden from the smallest seed. They are also amazed by rainbows, a turtle crossing the road or a kitten playfully chasing a string. Unlike children, some of us have long lost our enthusiasm about God's creation and His interesting one-of-a-kind creatures. Our lack of excitement is such a shame because God has created an extravagant universe, which is most stunning in its design.

Even though God's universe is beyond compare, the Creator is greater still. He is grander than the fastest comet. He is more majestic than the Milky Way or a soulful sunset painted in the heavens. If the beauty found on Earth is any indication of its Maker, then God is a glorious, radiant, colorful, pure Being who delights in showing us attributes of Himself so that we may marvel at who He is and desire to worship Him. He wants us to constantly acknowledge that He alone is capable of the creation of the universe; and in viewing that universe we should never lose sight of Him, the ultimate Creator and loving God.

In God's love, He placed man who He created in His Own Image,[8] to rule over this magnificent planet we call Earth. When God created Adam and Eve from the dust of the ground and blew His very own breath into their nostrils, He began the human bloodline that continues today.[9] He gave humans the ability to reproduce, and in so doing, He enabled the bloodline to continue. This bloodline traces our origins from Adam to Jesus Christ to every person conceived until this very minute. God's handiwork is further displayed in each of us because He uniquely fashions each person in His image, with that original divine bloodline as he forms us in our mother's womb.[10] God not only did this magnificent work, but He also recorded a portion of this amazing true story in the Bible. He has documented His account of human history for our instruction and His glory. Within the pages of His Word, God not only told us about the people and the animals He created, but He has also revealed His nature, His character and His love for man. He shows us that we are living in the middle of His story, and He is also gracious to give us a glimpse of what will come in the future. He has told us how we began, how the story will end and how we are to live in between.

Despite the fact that we are made in His image and that we have been given His Living Word as a roadmap for an abundant life, we sometimes still manage to lose our compass as we walk along the journey of life. Maybe we stray because of life's pressures, or perhaps we get off course because of our strong desire to please ourselves or others. As we go our own way, we can wander from the absolute Truth found in our Creator's Guidebook, which then, in turn, makes us prone to cling to whatever is culturally relative. Then, this relativism encourages us to form our own opinions. Finally, we begin to make the mistake that we can use these opinions to decide who God is. However, God will not be defined. He is not who we determine He is, but He is who He says He is.[11] The only way we will ever have an understanding of any topic is to go to the Master of all things and see what His Word has to say about the subject.

---

[8] Genesis 1:27
[9] Genesis 2:7
[10] Psalm 139:13–14
[11] Isaiah 43:10; Exodus 3:14

If you wanted to help someone really understand you, wouldn't you find a way to tell them? God has done that. He wrote down who He is and what He does in His Book, the Bible. He even tells us how to use this crucial resource. He says that we need to seek God to discover Him. Seeking is not skimming pages or half-halfhearted attempts of understanding. It is not reading God's Word only when we feel like it or when we think we have the time. Discovering Him is an ongoing determination to understand the truth in the Bible—at all cost—no matter how long it takes. We must dedicate time to cultivate and discover this biblical understanding on a daily basis if we want to live with peace that isn't contingent on our circumstances. Without accurate biblical understanding, we cannot intimately know our Father God in a continuous, loving relationship that removes any doubt about His ongoing love—a love that is always present even in the face of difficult circumstances. The love that created the universe and the human race is the same love that placed Jesus on the cross. The love that created all the animals is the same love that wants us to also know the truth of the Father's love for us.

What are we giving up by ignoring the great knowledge and Truth found in God's Word? We are giving up wisdom available from a gracious, all-loving God that enables us to know and receive Jesus Christ. Knowing Christ intimately leads to a peaceful, abundant life here on earth. Sadly, if we have never taken the time to discover God's truth about Jesus and to formulate an authentic relationship with Him, we could also be deceived into thinking we are Heaven bound only to discover—when it is too late—that we were wrong. Proverbs 1:7 says, "The fear of the Lord is the beginning of knowledge, But fools despise wisdom and instruction." To refuse, rebuke or ignore God's wisdom and instruction will bring destruction, distress and anguish. He will refuse to listen to our desperate cries if we remain stubborn and refuse to listen to His warning. But, if we listen to Him, we will dwell in safety and be secure without fear. God as the Apron is where our security lies, in the very arms of God who started it all. It is that simple. Rediscover Him in a relationship where His Apron will enable us to receive all of the blessings he has for us in this life. His Apron will also guard us from dismissing the truths God has placed in the Bible to guide our lives. With the Apron wrapped around us, we have a better understanding about how God works in this world, what a person devoted to God acts like, and how to allow His Truth to be our Shield.[12]

---

[12] Psalm 91: 1–4

Tying God's Apron Strings Around Your Heart

Visit the zoo, a farm or simply take a long walk. What do you notice about the majesty of God in creation? Can you see His handiwork? What does spending time exploring nature tell you about His faithfulness? Or how does it show you that He made everything work together for good, providing for it all? Then, take a moment to stop and thank God that He enables you to discover His provision and how in seeing it He allows you to glimpse into His heart. Let the beauty of what you see cause you to want to discover even more about Him and worship Him more because He alone is worthy of your praise.

Chapter 3
Sharpener

As iron sharpens iron, So a man sharpens the countenance of his friend.
Proverbs 27:17, NKJV

On a summer day in our town, I can hear an auctioneer for miles around. The auctioneer uses almost a chanting tone as he scans the crowd for a bidder of an item with questionable value. As usual, my husband—drawn into the auction by this booming voice—has searched every bin, box and wood shed to find any little treasure for which he might have some use, any use. He, unlike some, is not looking for a diamond in the rough; he is just seeking something that he can convince me that we have suffered long enough without. A case in point was the time he purchased a knife set. As our daughter put it, the knife set was a tetanus shot waiting to happen. "But these are the best knives ever made," my husband said in his defense. I think someone should have told the previous owner how great they were because I am pretty sure they were just retrieved from a dust covered box in a shed without a door. I can see the box laying there in my mind's eye—littered with leaves and acorns.

We arrive home with our newly gained culinary paraphernalia, which I promptly washed and conveniently hid in the junk drawer. Within a few days, my better half was questioning the whereabouts of his most recent acquisition. I reluctantly pulled the set from its tomb, and he proudly displayed the knives in their ancient looking knife holder.

I admit I was simply biased toward my lovely shiny knives. I wanted no part of those dingy wooden handle versions. No manner of washing could improve their appearance, and my bigotry continued. Yes, that's right—I am a knife bigot. But, on a day when every dish in the house was dirty and I needed a knife, the only ones left were those with whom I have refused companionship. There it was: the last knife in the holder. I slowly picked it up and scanned it begrudgingly. Why, to my surprise, the ugly duckling sliced like a dream! I couldn't believe it! How could something that looked so bad be so good? Needless to say, the old steel regained a little respect that day. I recently told my husband how surprised I was that the knives were still sharp after such extended use. He decided right then and there to get out his next to newest gadget—a knife sharpener. He sharpened all but one of his treasured knives. The one that was missed was hiding in the sink. How nice, I thought, these old babies will cut even better. Boy was I wrong. They wouldn't cut a good stick of butter!

He had used the right tool—or so he thought. But the tool was apparently lacking. That's what happens when we trust any source but the Bible for the sharpening of our spiritual skills. The more we read sources other than the Bible or Christian books that reflect biblical teaching, the duller we become. We may think that because a book is a bestseller or because it is intellectual that if we believe it and use it, then we will be using the right tool. But, under closer examination, we may find that many of the ideas reflected in that book are in direct opposition to God's biblical Truth. To believe something that opposes God's Truth is to stand in opposition to God Himself—and that is akin to trying to use a dull knife to cut a thick piece of meat. You aren't going to get the much needed strength and nutrition that meat would give because you will have to leave the meat at the table. You will have already become full choosing something that won't really nourish you adequately.

It's unfortunate that all my knives became dull. However, it is grievous when we allow something to guide us besides God. As with the knives, our spiritual senses over time become duller and duller. We make less and less impact for His Kingdom and more and more impact for the other side. When I was a teenager, I allowed myself to be dull because I compromised my biblical stand for the prevailing winds of the day. I believed that premarital sex was okay if you really love the person. Because I did not take a firm stand against premarital sex, I was actually condoning it. I told myself that because I was not sleeping around that it was okay to believe it was fine for others to do what they wanted. After all, what harm would that do? But the harm was that because I did not take a strong mental stand on this particular issue, when other temptations came my way, it was easier for me to fall into other areas of sin. I did fall into materialism and self-sufficiency. I allowed my spiritual senses to become dull and I neglected my relationship with God. I was not living according to what the Bible teaches. I wonder if my friends who fell prey to sexual heartbreak prior to marriage would have been better protected if I had been sharper and taken a stand for biblical truth. I will never know. What I do know and have learned is that our dullness will leave us and those around us unprotected and unfed, and that is why I have started speaking out. Today, I choose to believe God, whether it is socially acceptable or not.

I am comforted by the truth that no matter where we have been or what we did yesterday, we can choose today to put on the Apron of God's protection and sharpen our spiritual senses by spending time in prayer, reading the Word and being in community with others who are dedicated to staying sharp. Tying the Apron strings in these ways will sharpen us with godly confidence because we have guarded ourselves against sinful ripples of compromise and conformity.

Tying God's Apron Strings Around Your Heart

In what ways do you feel spiritually dull? Have you asked God to sharpen you? Maybe God would like to grow your gentleness, help you persevere in patience, or give you victory over an ongoing sin? Whatever clutter needs to be cut out of your life, God has the right tool for the job. Take a few moments to go to God in prayer asking Him to show you where you need to be sharpened. Listen carefully and open your heart to receive and act upon His instruction.

Chapter 4
Focus

"Go therefore and make disciples of all the nations, baptizing them in the name of the Father and of the Son and of the Holy Spirit, teaching them to observe all things that I have commanded you; and lo, I am with you always, even to the end of the age."
Matthew 28:19–20, NKJV

I see an unfamiliar vehicle pull into our short, dusty driveway. The vehicle's occupants have parked at the very end of the driveway without actually blocking the road. This action tells me they either plan a very short stay or that they need a clean getaway. Since I knew my children were on the premises, I kept a hawkish eye upon the unknown visitor. Many times people are startled when they step upon the porch to find a person starring at them from the other side of the screen door.

When I saw that my unsolicited guest was an elderly woman, I didn't want to frighten her. So, I stepped outside the door as soon as she could see me. I greeted her cordially because I did not know her, nor did I have an inkling of what business motivated her visit. After the usual Southern pleasantries about her health, her family's health and the condition of the weather, she got down to business. Her request was met with my rebuff. I gently declined her offer to accept a newsletter explaining everything she felt I needed to know about the destruction of the world. Then, a more familiar person approached—my neighbor. She is a sweet tempered woman with a genuine smile and a nicely arranged covering of gray hair. Her face was slightly weathered by what appeared to be excessive sun exposure that reminded me of her Western heritage. Her companion, the elderly lady, had finally given up her mission of convincing me to see the light, leaving my neighbor to continue the task. My neighbor was refuting something I had stated and was showing evidence in the Bible to prove her point. I understand the practice quite well and stopped her to ask this question. "Why, when I have kindly stated my relationship to Jesus do you persist in trying to convince me of some error in judgment?" She had no explanation, and without allowing any lengthy thought on the matter, she continued without hesitation.

I am always amazed at the sheer volume of interpretations of the same book. It is human nature to have differences of opinions, I guess. But, many times our interpretations are tainted by our own life experiences and what we have been taught. My thoughts were not argumentative; I never tried to prove what I felt was correct. I simply wanted them to accept my devotion to Jesus and lay the matter to rest. But, they could not let it go. I was not part of their denomination. God does not segregate His Kingdom, but here in the South, segregation must still be a big deal. It isn't based on the color of skin, but segregation lives on between denominations and congregations. Many believe if someone is not a member of a particular church denomination or congregation, then he or she must be in error. This segregation is possibly a byproduct of people in churches spending so much time arguing about denominations that collectively none of them has taken enough time to go and tell those who don't know Jesus about His saving grace. In general, many people are not focused on sharing the hope of Christ, which is one of the main reasons we have an organized body called the Church.

I have been a grieved witness seeing the horror of a family member who found out that their loved one was attending church in a congregation of which they did not approve. Unhappiness and pressure about the error of these spiritual choices grew so much in the family that the family member who had just begun visiting church stopped attending church altogether. It bewilders me that anyone would rather have their loved one not attend church at all and subsequently reduce their hope of knowing Jesus simply because they had visited a church whose name did not match their own particular persuasion. It didn't matter that the objecting family member didn't live for Jesus or appear dedicated to their denomination of choice. In this particular instance, family members weren't happy until they had thwarted any chance of their loved one hearing about Jesus anywhere else. I must say, this internal division of a family keeping someone created by God away from church is Satan doing his finest work.

Let me pause here to interject that not all religious organizations teach that Jesus is the only way to Heaven. Concern for others is warranted if they became affiliated with a group that does not preach and teach the undiluted Word of God. However, none of us should take what we are taught on face value, even if it sounds biblically correct. It is our job to verify what we and our children are being taught with the Word of God. Even a God-fearing preacher or teacher can make a mistake. But, we must not allow that mistake to take root and cause confusion or inadvertent disobedience. The possibility of errant teaching is another reason that God calls us to read our Bible daily. Failure to check what we hear against the truth in God's Word can cause a malnourished soul. Instead of getting a daily dose of vitamin Bible, we could be getting a heaping spoonful of false teaching. We will never be healthy maturing Christians if we are not studying biblical truth with the desire to learn and apply its principles.

Far too many times we may become too focused on our own church denomination or even one specific body of believers. We are prone to forget that we are instructed by Jesus to work together rather than hindering other people that God has placed on this planet to also reach lost souls. We need to spend less time putting other churches down. We need to stop trying to sway members away from other churches. Instead, we need to focus our efforts, spending more time building God's Kingdom by loving others and telling them more about Jesus.

Because many people in the church neglect God's command to share the Gospel, they may be stuck in a literal rut and never seem to move forward. I am afraid we have been sitting around chewing the cud,[13] so to speak. Meantime, nothing of real Kingdom value is getting done. As a result, the outside world has been starving. People have been seeking fulfillment in all the wrong places instead of where satisfaction really lies—in God's Truth. A significant gap exists where the work that God wanted to do through us could have been accomplished. People who don't yet know Christ intimately have been left to wonder which church is correct. They don't understand why we can't get along since we all claim to have the same Master.

It is no wonder that so few people—including Christians—are interested in what God has to say. Even Christians are prone to not hear Him through all the static caused by the complaining and finger pointing. I am afraid we have lost our focus. The focus on God's Kingdom is eclipsed by the focus on our particular church. The focus we should have on God and lost people is dwarfed by the other minor interests of our particular congregation. We need to be less concerned with recruiting

---

[13] Discussing and mulling things over and over for a long period of time

members for our churches and return to the work of making disciples. The difference is in the focus.[14]

I realized during my season of anxiety attacks that my focus hadn't been on God, but that focus on Him is the nutritional infusion that we all need. To focus on God, we need to be nourished by His Presence. Let us return to His table, eat His food and put on the protection of the Apron. His Apron shields those who wear it, and enables them to become royal priests.[15] Priests, in turn, work in the power of Christ, to create unity for the greater good of all mankind. The protection of the Apron will guard His faithful priests and all Christ followers by keeping the world from seeping through the cracks of our church walls. The Apron keeps us from being distracted by our sometimes narrow or distorted view of God's mission. This Apron also enables us to endure difficulty as we, by faith, speak the truth to those who do not yet know Him.

Tying God's Apron Strings Around Your Heart

Could your focus on sharing your faith with people who don't know Jesus be stronger? Do you have any disagreements within your family or in your circle of influence that may be preventing others from knowing Jesus? Ask God to help you to be more bold with those who don't know Jesus. Ask God to help you love others where they are so that there is hope that they will hear more about Jesus and embrace Him. As you love others who may have different beliefs than you do, ask God to help you have His mind and heart, so that you lovingly share the truth of Jesus.

---

[14] Mark 9:39–41
[15] 1 Peter 2:9

Chapter 5
Mistaken Identity

For thus says the LORD, *Who created the heavens, Who is God, Who formed the earth and made it, Who has established it, Who did not create it in vain, Who formed it to be inhabited:*
"I am the LORD, *and there is no other."*
Isaiah 45:18, NKJV

It is a sunny but breezy fall morning and my husband feels that we should visit the stock barn in the next town over with our two youngest children. He says that it will be a nice outing for the boys. I think he just wants to buy more chickens. Regardless, I agree and prepare myself for additional animals if the price is right. We arrive and walk on the elevated platform so we may see everything great and small that is for sale. We finally find a seat on the wooden bleachers. I see many families sitting together, snacking on items purchased at the concession stand. The auctioneer begins his chanting and everyone's attention is diverted to the center arena where the animals are about to be shown. Throughout the day we see several different species. We see everything from grand champion rabbits to your everyday, run of the mill, barnyard chickens. Grand champions have an air about them because of many hours in training but barnyard varieties are only interested in demonstrating the skills for which God has equipped them. They don't care where they do their business nor are they particular about where it might land.

Humans can have an air about them too. Just after the midway point of one of the sales, a commotion occurs in front of the fence keeping the humans and animals separated. A little boy wearing denim overalls, a flannel shirt and cowboy boots is raising quite a ruckus. A grand champion rabbit is up for auction and it is obvious the child wants this treasure. The bid rose to $25 before interest ceased. The owner, who was handling the rabbit on the main floor, informed the auctioneer of a no sale. She would not accept the bid. It was too low for her winning animal.

Her rock bottom price was $75. The parents sheepishly declined. That's when the wailing began. Not a single man nor beast in the barn could have missed the attitude and the scream of this little cowboy. As you might have guessed, the verdict was overturned, the rabbit was purchased for the owners asking price and the fuss was over as quickly as it began. I must say this is the best child-trained parent I have ever seen. I hope my surprise was not as noticeable as I think it might have been because my jaw dropped for several seconds after seeing this spectacle. Whether the animal was needed or affordable did not matter. The child wanted it and that was the end of it. No thought was placed on rewarding bad behavior or how this appeasement would affect him later on when he wanted something that was impossible to get.

I am afraid that we as children of God have the same idea that this mother and child did. We think as children that we are in charge. We think that we know what is best. Somehow God is mistakenly thought of as a fairy godmother or genie in a bottle here for our wish-making delight. We only call upon him when we are in trouble and need bailing out. Then, we send Him back to wherever He comes from, and we continue to live our life as we please. That is, we live our life without Him until the next time that we think we need His assistance.

God is not here to give us everything we want. In essence, He is continually training us to be more like His Son. He is equipping us for our next life—you know—the one we will have in Heaven. Many times we are like the child who wanted the rabbit. When God won't immediately give us what we ask for, we try to find our own way, and it starts with us throwing a grown-up fit finer than any two year old could muster. Even though the ruckus we raise may not stem from wanting an animal, it is nonetheless childish. We don't bother trying to see our outburst from God's perspective. We don't think about how the object of our intense desire could hinder us later on. We don't pray and ask Him to reveal His plan and enable us to calmly wait. We say or think to ourselves, "I'll show God! I'll stop going to church because I don't want to see Him! I won't pray because I don't want to talk to Him! I won't give Him any of my money because it's mine and not His!"

When God doesn't answer us immediately, He is letting us know that it is good for us to learn to wait and share. Waiting on the Lord will give us strength and courage to persevere when life gets too hard.[16] Hebrews 13:16 urges us not to forget to do good and to share because it pleases God. As I thought about sharing in my own life, I have noticed

---

[16] Psalm 27:14; Isaiah 40:31

that sharing keeps greed and desire to control at bay. Willingness to give away time, talents or resources to help another requires a mindset that says, "I am willing to sacrifice so that another may have their needs met. It's not all about me." God knows sharing is a sacrifice. He knows that it is hard for us. But He tells us up front that the sacrifice is pleasing to Him. Sharing is an aspect of loving.[17] And let's not forget, Jesus said love for our neighbor is one of the greatest commandments.

It won't harm us if we don't get what we want. If we can learn to be content with what God is choosing to give us for this season of our life, we will ward off unnecessary discouragement and unhappiness. Life is so much richer with contentment because we are choosing to have joy regardless of our circumstances.[18] No matter what we are facing in life, we are told in the Bible to ask God what He thinks and to submit to His Authority. How will we ever learn to wait on God and accept when He says,"No," if we never practice that skill? How will we learn to allow God to be in charge?

God has all authority.[19] His true identity is that He is the creator and supreme ruler of the universe.[20] He commands Heaven and Earth. He has complete control over life and death.[21] He has all the power! He never has to ask permission. He never has to investigate, and He doesn't negotiate about what He says about what is sin.

If we have had a mistaken impression of who God is, it will take some time in prayer and in studying God's Word asking our Heavenly Father to help us to truly recognize his authentic role and to accept His sovereignty. When we accept who He is, we will receive an infusion of spiritual nourishment. Understanding who He is and accepting that will allow God, with His Apron to shield us from greed, selfishness and an unloving attitude toward others. What we will gain instead under His protection is a stronger trust in the God of the universe. A few less emotional breakdowns might be avoided if we would simply understand God's authority. He makes the rules. We do not. He is God and we are not. He will help us clearly see Him as God and ourselves as His children if we let Him. As our vantage point becomes more and more clear, we will experience fewer cases of spiritual mistaken identity.

---

[17] Mark 12:31
[18] 1 Timothy 6:6; Philippians 4:11
[19] Matthew 28:18
[20] Genesis 1:1; Psalm 90:2
[21] Jeremiah 1:5; Psalm 139:16

Tying God's Apron Strings Around Your Heart

Are there areas of your life where you are throwing a spiritual temper tantrum? Are you trying too hard to get something that you think you must have to survive? Many of us have something we are striving for most of the time. But God offers us peace and promises to provide everything we need when we seek Him. Ask Him to conform your will to His, because He knows what is best for you. He knows what is best for us to do and not do. Record your thoughts and pray with a trusted friend about these truths.

Chapter 6
The Race

"For My thoughts are not your thoughts, Nor are your ways My ways," says the Lord. "For as the heavens are higher than the earth, So are My ways higher than your ways, And My thoughts than your thoughts."
Isaiah 55:8, NKJV

It is Saturday and my family and I are enjoying a much needed lunch break. We have stopped in at our favorite fast food restaurant and are enjoying a meal of all the best comfort food down to the milkshake and fries. My husband looks at me and says, "Go and order another meal." Instead of refusing to listen to the voice in his heart, he responds. He knows God has a plan. Someone has a need; the way God will meet that need is through His people. On this Saturday, God made this request for another meal to the Stone family. It was simple. We were to purchase a meal and deliver it to a hungry man. Even though we did not know for whom the food was intended, God knew.

We finished our lunch and left with the extra meal in hand. Just as we prepared to stop at the first intersection after we drove away from the restaurant, we saw a veteran on our right wearily sitting on the ground with a faded green backpack at his side. We pulled over and my husband asked," Have you eaten today?" The man was hesitant to answer. But my husband placed the to-go bag in his hand. The stranger grabbed it and immediately began to consume the food with such intensity that it was obvious he had not eaten in quite a while. The stranger made one last gingerly reach for some much needed refreshment as my husband placed a tall cup of sweet tea in the stranger's hand. The man was grateful. Maybe he couldn't say it. But, it showed all over his wind-burnt face. His only reply was, "Why?"

"Thank you for your service," my husband said. We moved on and never saw him again. We didn't have to know who he was or to understand his story. We only knew that God had an assignment for us. We listened when God spoke and responded in obedience.

Have you ever taken time to look around at all the people rushing everywhere? It is like we are in a race, literally. We can't even be still long enough to enjoy a meal or a cup of coffee. That is why there are so many drive-thru windows and fast food restaurants. We eat on the go, study on the go, groom ourselves on the go and build relationships on the go. We miss out on so much because we are not running the race God has set before us. We are running our own shows. God's charge, however, would be for us to slow down so that we could see His work in the world. Slowing down would give us the time to join Him when He invites us to partner with Him in His work. His pace is steady and sure. It makes room for the unexpected. As we walk with Him at His pace, we will have time to notice those around us who are hurting. Some people just need a smile or kind word to know that God cares about them. I have had those moments when I knew God wanted me to take the time for His agenda and not mine. God's pace allows time for prayer when we or someone we meet needs it, even if it will cause a delay in our preplanned schedule. God's agenda tells us to share what we know about Jesus so that others can also have hope. What could be more important than God's plan for the day?

The Bible says we are to run the race in such a way that we obtain the prize.[22] God does not want us to run so we may beat the next person. He wants us to keep our focus on Him, allowing Him to help us, while we live out our belief in Jesus. To win the prize, which is our relationship to Him and subsequently Heaven, we will have to run with endurance. Enduring unpleasant circumstances without giving up, will—at times—require us to slow down and refocus on God. This act of refocusing will help us match His pace allowing us to finish well rather than finishing first.

Sometimes obstacles in our life hinder us from staying in step with God's pace. Our tendency to rush keeps our mind distracted from the things of God. Many of us have packed so much into our lives that we are constantly worn out and our nerves are frazzled. Exhaustion and worry can create a very disagreeable person. I know, because before my anxiety attacks, I was often exhausted and worried, and somewhat disagreeable. As Christians, though, we are called to have the mind of

---

[22] 1 Corinthians 9:24

Christ and remain composed when others aren't. We are told to draw strength from Him and take the high road and make the hard choices. The normal pattern of a consistently hurried lifestyle leaves little room for godly living. It took my family being refined through my season of anxiety and other challenging events to slow down and listen to God. I pray you can learn from our experiences.

Today, in addition to being hurried and trying to engage in many activities all the time, many among us are also addicted to electronic gadgets. We can't sit in a restaurant with our family or friends without checking email or social media. Our children can't make a short trip to the grocery store without something to watch or play. And we certainly don't want them to. The gadgets help keep them from saying, "Are we there yet?" or "I'm bored." Without these electronic distractions they might actually have to learn to get along with a real human instead of just engaging in a game. They might have to interact with each other by building a relationship with a sibling or a friend.

Speaking of building relationships, another reason we need to slow down and live at the pace and course that God calls us to is that we have precious few moments together on this planet. Our lives are—in the larger scheme of things—very short.[23] The brevity of life makes me wonder why people may waste this priceless and nonrenewable commodity with electronics instead of on children, spouse or friends. We never get that time back again. It is lost forever. We need to make the most of it. If we are too busy in the evening to turn off our phone, television or computer for even an hour to invest in our family, then we are simply too busy. If our hectic schedule hinders church attendance or Bible study, we have placed something before God and the race we are running does not lead to Him. If we are on the wrong track, we will not obtain the prize of a relationship with God Himself.

By putting on God's Apron through prayer and listening to the Holy Spirit, we are given the presence of mind to build relationships with others now. God's Apron offers us the protection of saving ourselves from the regret that could come at the end of our lives when we might look back and say, "I wish I would have spent more time with my children while they were at home. I wish I would have enjoyed time with my parents while they were alive. I wish I had just one more sunset with my spouse."

---

[23] James 4:14

God, in His grace, has taught me to stay on course in terms of making the most of special memories with my loved ones. He helps me orchestrate occasions at the table to intentionally create connections and memories. One such time was with my grandmother near the end of her life when my dad brought her to our home for a family meal fresh from our garden. It was a special bonding time for us because my grandmother was married to a farmer and she loved gardening and canning just like I do. She just about ate every last fried green tomato that we cooked that day. I still remember her smile as she looked at me and said, "That is the best meal I have had in a while." I remember her each year as we plant and harvest our garden. She seemed to have a great time that day as we sat on the front porch and talked about times gone by. She held her great-great-grandchild for the first and last time. She was insistent that she feed him and we were all worried she was too frail to hold him. But, she was a determined woman, and she found a way and it was obvious she relished every moment.

Because I have learned to seize significant moments like my grandmother did, when my father was very sick before he died, God had prompted me to go see my father three times in one day, and I went. While I was with him, I read the local newspaper out loud. He was miserably sick, but asked me to keep reading to him until every article had been read. Later that day as I fed him, he was almost giddy with delight; he was very much like a child. I am comforted now by the fact God prompted me to use every available moment that day to spend time with him. I am certain that God led me to take advantage of these precious moments because they were rapidly coming to an end. These special times went a long way in helping me not have regrets after my father's death. I praise God that during those last few days of my loved ones' lives, I was not too busy running my race to hear His nudges prompting me to make treasured memories.

If we will put on and keep on God's Apron, we will live at God's pace, allow for His intentional pauses and special moments, relish our time with Him and others, and never look back in regret. We will satisfy our souls, knowing that we lived abundantly. We can say with confidence that we took advantage of every moment God gave us because tomorrow wasn't promised. We made the most of each day. We allowed ourselves to be the hands and feet of God. I want to hear Him say, "Well done, good and faithful servant…enter into the joy of your Lord." Don't you?

Tying God's Apron Strings Around Your Heart

Do you feel like you are running on overload? If so, I encourage you to slow down, and move at God's pace. Try to take an extra 30 minutes each day to just be still and to know that He is God. Ask Jesus to show you how fast he is moving, so that you can be in step with Him. If you haven't had a special time with loved ones lately, ask God to help you to take time to create regular special moments with those you cherish. Finally, take an honest look to see if you are chained to your gadgets. If so, ask God to help you break free and turn them off for at least a couple hours each day.

Chapter 7
Trust

*Trust in the L*ORD *with all your heart, And lean not on your own understanding; In all your ways acknowledge Him, And He shall direct your paths.*
Proverbs 3:5–6, NKJV

I still struggle with balancing my life. This juggling act is not easy. I remember when God showed me the obstacles that kept me anxious and overwhelmed because my trust was misplaced. Our family had just moved into a 106-year-old Southern antebellum home. I could see the beauty that lay just beneath the surface. It just needed a little tender-loving care—or so I thought. Although the major renovation is now behind us, we still spend quite a bit of time repairing and replacing the home's features. We have been in the process of making it our own without sacrificing the integrity of the home. We want it to have a personal touch that helps us embrace this experience we call life. Early on in the renovation, because of our limited budget, we had to survive without a television, the Internet or a cell phone. It was during this time that I began to see how so much of my spare time was tied up using electronics. I previously felt that I did not have time to study God's Word or pray. It quickly became abundantly clear that the time was there; I had just been a poor steward of it. I had not trusted God with my time. I did not put Him first.

During this time without access to TV or Internet, I also became aware of how much I had previously been consumed with the need to constantly know more. I realized that I had let fear of not knowing enough overtake me. After a few months without television, I found that I was less fearful about life in general. That's because so much of the news on TV contains an element of fear. As we watch the news, we develop fear about crime, health, inappropriate education, dangerous weather and catastrophic financial practices. God, however, does not intend for us to live in fear. Without a television or the Internet in my home, I had to learn to rely on God without knowing what was happening in our world every minute of the day. It caused me to focus more on Him and on other relationships in my life. My mind was no longer constantly thinking about something I had seen or dreading what might happen. God had removed that obstacle—rather that disturbance—that hindered my trust in Him. He had to remove the junk in my mind to make room for more of Jesus. As I let more of the truth of Jesus in, the more I experienced trusting Him.

Since then, God has proven his trustworthiness to me many times over, but, I was blown away by his faithfulness when I had to travel somewhere unfamiliar without a cell phone. Anxiety stricken and determined to persevere, I left home. I remember at one point pulling over on the shoulder of the road and immediately praying. I asked the Lord to help me trust Him. I knew that He could protect me and help me get to my destination. I needed help with my doubt. I needed help with my nerves. I needed help with my faith. My head knew God was capable, but my heart didn't know if He would help me. I was not willing to give up, however. I would have to trust Him. I arrived at my destination and back home much calmer than when I had departed. That situation alone showed me that I had trusted in my phone more than I had trusted in God. My cell phone does not have the power to save my life, but God does. I learned that I can live without my cell phone. But, I can't live without God.

Because we naturally don't want to slow down to see what God might be doing, we tend to rush and move without godly discernment to get matters resolved ourselves. We are in a hurry to get tasks done so that we can move on to the next item on our list. God is more concerned about quality than speed. He wants to build a relationship with us so that we trust Him and He wants us to build our relationships with others as well. As we travel through life, God calls us, who claim to be His, to learn to trust His ways even if we don't understand them. If we are willing, He will give us the courage and strength to walk with Him because of His promise that He will never leave us to stumble on our own in this world of fear and darkness.[24] If we are willing, He will show us how to walk joyfully, triumphantly and bravely regardless of our circumstances. Putting on God's Apron and trusting Him to guide our steps will relieve anxiety about the future and the great unknown. Wearing His Apron will

---

[24] Deuteronomy 31:6

help us remember that we are never alone. It will help us set our pace, and have the peace that passes all understanding even in the midst of chaos.[25] We will experience joy and fulfillment, and life without fear. Now that's nourishment.

Tying God's Apron Strings Around Your Heart

Is focusing too much on world news and being informed diminishing your trust in God? If so, it may be time to scale back the time you spend hearing about the headlines and to dive deeper into the truth found in the Bible. God's Word will never be yesterday's news! If you are struggling to trust him in this ever-changing world, open up the Word of God and do a word study on trust. Ask God to help you trust him in a greater way, and ask Him to keep showing you his trustworthiness. I also encourage you to read a story about one of the many times God was faithful to deliver His people from calamity. One of my personal favorites is the story of Esther. God is such a mighty deliverer!

---

[25] Philippians 4:6–7

Chapter 8
Alert

Therefore, with minds that are alert and fully sober, set your hope on the grace to be brought to you when Jesus Christ is revealed at his coming.
1 Peter 1:13, NIV

As children of God, we are called to participate in activities that honor and glorify Him. That action necessitates prioritizing our lives to make room for Him and to know His rules. We need to avoid huge time wasters and understand that what we watch or listen to can be offensive to God. In short, to revere God, we need to be alert about what we put into our minds.

As you know, what goes into our minds ultimately comes out into our lives somewhere. As parents or friends, we can try to set godly examples in every way. All our efforts can be in vain when some ungodly thought or action comes out unexpectedly. No matter how much progress we have made in our spiritual lives, we always have room for improvement. One area of growth might be the amount of time you spend with God. Even if you have a time set aside for Him, how does that amount of time compare to the amount of time and energy you spend on other activities? I challenge you to find out. Test your household: How much time is spent studying the Bible and praying compared to the time spent on other pursuits? You can even include the time spent at church on God's side of the equation. I think that most people will be amazed to see how much the actual amount of time spent in activities purely for our own self-interest far outweighs the time spent growing our relationship with God. This exercise is important because what we say that we believe is either validated or voided by how we live. What we allow ourselves to be exposed to, if not in line with Scripture, can hinder and contradict the time spent at home or church learning about God. If we are not careful, we will be drawn away by the temptations we encounter. We need to pay close attention to what we read, watch and do with our free time. To honor God, we must measure our activities by the truth in God's Word. If an activity doesn't glorify God, then it needs to go!

Let me ask you a question, if I may. Would you allow a half-naked person under the influence of alcohol or drugs to lounge on your sofa with your family for the evening? Would you invite people over to make out with your children in the room? Probably not. These activities would—if you're like many of my Southern lady friends—make you uncomfortable. But we have no qualms about watching these same scenes in a movie, on the Internet or even reading about such shenanigans in a book. We have just invited whatever is happening in these media into our homes and into our minds. Somehow we are not offended by these mind games. Maybe our lack of offense is because we think that no one sees what we watch, hear or read because it is behind closed doors. God, however, sees. And He is offended by this deceitfulness.[26]

I have heard it said that if we want to watch television we will just have to put up with ungodly behavior. I beg to differ. The world we live in is driven by power and greed. If we stop watching, ratings go down. If ratings go down, changes in program content are made. If we stop spending money on items or activities that God does not approve of, changes will be made. Wherever money is made, you can guarantee that a company somewhere is going to want that piece of the pie. Companies may not care as much about what they sell as long as it sells. So if we are only interested in buying things that honor and please God, then changes would have to be made if these companies want to earn our business. The problem is we don't change our behavior. "It's too much trouble to bother," some would say. "It will cost more for something different," another might add. We might have to wait. These excuses don't measure up as reasons for not honoring God with our actions and attitudes. If the activity doesn't honor God, it isn't worth the precious time in our lives.

As we learn more about God and his character, He changes our perspective and we are alerted to facets of our life that He would not approve of. We must then take this new-found awareness and make changes to our actions accordingly. Our minds should always be

---

[26] Philippians 4:8; Psalm 101:7; Hebrews 4:13

meditating on things that honor God.[27] This conscious meditation requires spiritual alertness motivated by a desire to please our Heavenly Father.

If you are feeling sad, confused or overwhelmed right about now, don't be discouraged. I have struggled with the same temptations using media. I believed the images I wanted to watch on television wouldn't permeate my mind, that the lyrics to unedifying music wouldn't sink into my soul, or that the words of a novel—that was just for an escape— wouldn't influence my thoughts. But I was nudged by the Holy Spirit to give these things up. It seemed unfair at first, but then I asked God for help. Do you know what I learned? I discovered that God will help us change our minds and hearts about our activities if we ask Him to. The first step, though, is to stop justifying our actions by saying that God doesn't care about some of this stuff when He really does. We tell ourselves that He doesn't care because it makes us feel better. But the more I read His Word, the more I know He is offended by ungodly behavior. He is concerned about what His children see or hear. But, don't take my word for it—read the Bible and see for yourself.

As we dig in God's Word, or put on God's Apron, He will protect us with a constant stream of godly information to nourish our minds and keep us focused on Him. This biblical nourishment—as we internalize it—will bring us peace and praiseworthy behavior that is pleasing to God. We will be less tempted because we are no longer allowing our mind to feast on the junk food of sexual content, profanity, unnecessary violence or the empty promises of materialism. God's Apron will ward off potential sinful behavior that can be fueled by seeing or watching such ungodly behaviors. Instead, we will experience the righteousness, peace and joy that comes from knowing and obeying our loving Father.

Tying God's Apron Strings Around Your Heart

Is God asking you to change some of your activities or entertainment? If so, ask Him to help you see how these activities may be influencing your behavior. Ask Him to remove the desire for anything that wouldn't be pleasing to Him. He will be faithful to change you as you continue to seek Him. Also ask Him to help you be alert to any deception that you may be harboring in your mind as a result of something you may have watched or an activity you may have engaged in at some time in the past. Pray that He will cleanse you from all unrighteousness, and know that He will wash you white as snow!

---

[27] Philippians 4:8–9

Chapter 9
Freedom

It is for freedom that Christ has set us free. Stand firm, then, and do not let yourselves be burdened again by a yoke of slavery.
Galatians 5:1, NIV

As I drive, I can see in my side mirror the small hand of my oldest grandchild. He had requested to roll down the car window and feel the wind between his fingers. I allowed him to do so. With his arm out the window, he turns his hand this way and that, up and down, side to side in a very slow swimming motion. His elbow rests on the half-open window, which helps his arm remain as high as he can reach for a good period of time. I didn't look back in my other mirror to know for sure, but I strongly suspected that his other hand was pressed against his lips with his thumb in his mouth. His uncle, who is also my oldest son, is still fairly young and enjoying this childhood whimsy as well. His neck is stretched as far out the window as the seat-belt will allow, and his hair is dancing erratically in an unpredictable waving motion. He keeps his chin held high and his teeth visible because he can't help but smile as the fresh country air billows across his handsome face. Both my son and my grandson appear as if their minds are fixed on some far off place. Or, maybe they are just embracing the sweetness of the moment and enjoying the simple pleasures that life has to offer. Feeling the air outside of the window brings a sense of freedom and peace transcending the realities of this world, transferring our minds to something beyond ourselves.

As adults, maybe we wonder if the peace and freedom felt in simple childhood adventures exist in a grown-up world. We question if we can find a place of release and escape from our troubles. As residents of Planet Earth in the 21st century, we live in a place where wars rage, hate drives persecution and illness and famine strike so many. Sometimes, as we consider what's happening in the world around us, that carefree childlike freedom fades to a dim recollection. I am here to say, however, that by God's grace, I have found that child-like peace. It is not a place or even a mindset. It is in my relationship with Jesus Christ. The Bible says, "Come you who are heavy laden and I will give you rest."[28] He came to save us and rescue us from worry, hopelessness, abandonment and eternal suffering. Jesus came to give us the ability to say as Horatio G. Spafford penned in his 1873 song, "It is Well With My Soul." Though wars and pestilence rage about me, "it is well with my soul." Why, because Jesus promises never to leave us nor forsake us.[29] He will never abandon us. He promises "good" to those who trust Him.[30] He has plans to prosper us and not harm us.[31] The Bible is full of these promises and many other verses showing us that God is trustworthy.

With the best resource—the Bible—readily available and often free, why are so many people taking anti-depressants, anti-anxiety medication or self-medicating with alcohol and drugs? One reason might be because they don't trust God. People may be self-destructing because they feel they have the right to do so. We as humans tend to want things to go our way even if our way is filled with regret, death and abuse—all of which leave us broken and empty. This emptiness we experience could leave us in a perpetual state of searching for something to fill it. Then some among us may use drugs—some even prescribed by our doctors—to numb our minds and emotions so that we may escape the pain that we feel.

Others may stimulate themselves sexually to induce pleasure because they want a new or additional sense of satisfaction out of life. We as people are desperately lonely and hopelessly want to feel loved and accepted. We may even search for someone to share a sexual experience with because we want to feel something, anything besides what we are feeling now. We may also search for a job title to give our life purpose and meaning to find additional fulfillment. All of these conquests often leave us feeling even emptier at the end of each day. We tend to fill our lives with enough meaningless activity to tell ourselves that our life is full. We may even believe our own lies for a while. But, when tragedy hits and we start to dwell on questions like "why" and think about "what might have been," reality sets in. We are broken. We are empty. We aren't

---

[28] Matthew 11:28
[29] Hebrews 13:5
[30] Lamentations 3:24–25
[31] Jeremiah 29:11

fulfilled. We are just busy, in a hurry, angry and tired. And so, the search for fulfillment goes on. We are caught in a cycle that leaves us less courageous and more defeated each time we pause to reflect.

Many cannot understand how God created us to need a Savior. Yes, we need saving. "What or whom do we need saving from?" you might ask. We need saving from ourselves, and from eternity without Christ. The only Savior is Jesus Christ. Without Him, we will continue to search until our dying day for something to fill the agonizing hole that only He can fill. Why are we so afraid of the one thing we need the most? We are afraid because we fear change. We fear the unknown and we fear losing control. The sad truth, though, is that we never had control to begin with. God is the only one in control.

I finally learned the lesson that I wasn't in control of my own life when God brought me to my knees through my bout with anxiety. As I couldn't function and sought medical advice, it was obvious that I had withdrawn from my life because of anxiety. I had no choice but to believe the doctors who thought that drugs would help. Instead, I found that on medication I felt even more disconnected by my drug-altered state of emotions. Fortunately, my counselor helped me with alternative strategies and I stopped taking medication within six months.

I found that my brokenness and anxiety caused me to cry out to God to find freedom. He delivered me and showed me that there is only one true Protector and Freedom Giver. He is the one true Apron. The Bible says He sets kings in their places and removes them as He pleases so I know that He is in control of everything even when I can't see it.[32]

I urge you today to recapture that childlike freedom that we talked about earlier. For some of you who had difficult childhoods, perhaps you will find that freedom today for the first time. That freedom can come as an adult by letting God have control of your life. Start by asking Him to forgive you of anything in your past or present that He would not approve of. Then tell Him you are tired of living life without Him. Ask Jesus to come into your heart and live. Now you are set to begin your new journey with peace and freedom, knowing that God will guide you every step of the way. He will also love you unconditionally, always. Be assured: You will live like never before if you will trust Him.

Maybe you have already trusted Jesus as your Savior. My question for you is, are you living in freedom for Him? Do you live like you believe

---

[32] Daniel 2:21; Romans 13:1

that everything in the Bible is absolutely true? Have you really given God control of your life? Maybe you answered these questions affirmatively. But you still wonder: "If I have really surrendered control to God, why is my life such a mess? Why don't I have peace about the future? Why do I worry so much?" We need to be careful that we aren't just relying on Jesus to provide a ticket out of Hell, but that we are surrendering every area of our lives to him. When we accept Him, it is as Lord AND Savior. A Lord rules and a Savior rescues.

Although we want to accept what Jesus has done, we don't seem to want to do our part on earth by obeying His commands. Jesus sacrificed his life by dying for the sins of all mankind. With this sacrifice, He made a way for us to escape the punishment of Hell. But, we don't want to sacrifice anything now for a brighter future later. He instructs us to sacrifice in order to have an abundant life of peace and joy here on earth. Accepting Him as ruler of our life and repeatedly remembering that we need Him as Savior ought to bring about maturity in our faith. If we did as He instructs us to do, we would stop being spiritual toddlers who have to be led around by the hand because we refuse to grow into adult Christians. What spiritual behavior resembles the actions of a toddler? I am glad you asked. If you have ever lived with a two-year-old child, you may not need this explanation. But for those who have missed this patience-building and temper-tantrum enduring clash of the wills between a parent and child, let me fill you in. Toddlers change their minds constantly and only want what they want when they want it. Similarly, spiritual toddlers are unsettled or undecided about their level of devotion to God. Many times they neglect church attendance, time dedicated to prayer and Bible study, which are all signs of spiritual immaturity. A human toddler has a limited ability to communicate and control their emotions. Spiritual immaturity can be marked by the lack of desire to know God better. Spiritual immaturity also manifests itself with an unconcerned attitude about what God is doing in the world and in the local church. Spiritual toddlers are not often interested in learning God's ways. Many times, they want to keep on living life on their own terms even after they say they have surrendered their life to Jesus.

Spiritual immaturity is also not marked by age or the length of time that has passed since you were saved. I myself was a toddler in the faith for 20 years. So, I know a little about refusing to grow up where God is concerned. God was drawing me, but I was ignoring His prompting to know Him better. I was also refusing to live in a way that says," I am completely, 100% sold out for Jesus." This partial acceptance or immaturity in our faith is one reason we are spiritually starving. We are choosing to go hungry when God has a feast laid out for us to enjoy. It is not God's plan for us to remain malnourished. God eventually got my attention through debilitating anxiety. It was then that I began to have freedom by partaking in His feast, and it was then that my attitude began to change so I could intentionally nourish myself with His high-quality spiritual food.

Adding spiritual nutrition to our diet spoon feeds us God's love, infusing it into our lives. These spiritual nutrients can then flow through us into the lives of others. All we need to do is to put on the Apron of His truth and grace. We need to commit fully to grow in our knowledge of God better and our desire to please Him will increase. What if God is just waiting, trying to show us how we could have freedom in Christ? We have the opportunity to soar with wings like eagles. As we fly, we would feel the wind of freedom on our faces, just like my boys did one sunny afternoon on the drive home.

Tying On His Apron Strings

Do you feel free or are you shackled by something that continuously restricts your ability to soar? Don't let your past or your present circumstances dictate your future. Jesus has already paid the price for freedom. But, are you willing to do your part by living a life surrendered daily to Him? Ask God to take you from where you are to where He wants you to be. Ask Him to remove any areas that might be keeping you in captivity. Ask Him for the strength not to go back to the familiar prison of any ungodly activity keeping you in bondage. Freedom awaits; don't let it pass you by.

Chapter 10
Compassion

But when He (Jesus) saw the multitudes, He was moved with compassion for them, because they were weary and scattered, like sheep having no shepherd.
Matthew 9:36, NKJV

The date for preschool graduation has been announced well in advance and has been on the calendar of parents and loved ones for quite a while. The preschoolers have practiced their walk across the stage and the actual day is finally here. Pictures of friends on the playground and children finger painting and signs with goals attained are hung on the wall where the slide show will be projected. After the wooden bleachers in the small gymnasium fill to capacity, the children's faces begin to appear in the dimly-lit space. Faces of every child reflect accomplishments throughout the year. Teachers stand ready to give certificates as students cross the stage with perfectly arranged hair and very shiny shoes. The small faces glow with pride as they hold their certificates in their hands. They look with excitement for family members, as they are unable to wait to show off their prizes. Most children seem so full of hope and are eager for the future as they talk about what they want to be when they grow up. The answers bring much laughter and an occasional "aw." Everyone knows the children have bright futures ahead of them.

Love, even the love of a child, can bring about emotion that drives us to do crazy things. Love keeps us awake at night wondering if the other person feels the same way. Love motivates us to deprive ourselves of sleep to comfort the sick. The love of a mother, a brother or even an aunt many of us understand; but what does the love of God, our Heavenly Father mean to us? I would venture to say that many misunderstand His love in our angry, self-absorbed society. We cannot fathom how God loves differently than we do.[33] He is not motivated by what motivates us.[34] He does not take pleasure in seeing someone get what we feel they deserve.

Our judgmental nature causes us to lack compassion for the suffering and the weak. Our selfish ways may cause us to look the other way when someone stands on the side of the road holding a cardboard sign or when a teenage mother is frustrated with her crying baby. We may assume some poor choice on their part has led them to where they are now. Maybe it was a poor choice that got them there; or maybe it wasn't. But, one thing is for sure: if it were not for the grace of Almighty God each of us could be in that person's desolate situation. I am sure no one plans to become the town drunk, a prostitute or the person in jail for embezzlement. You never hear about these or other difficult scenarios when children describe their hopes about their future lives during the preschool graduation. But, at some point, one thing led to another, and people's lives become a mess. We all are in the same boat; all of us are residents of Planet Earth constantly trying to survive. We are called to be compassionate and filled with the grace God gives each of us.

God enables me to show compassion to other stay-at-home moms because I can relate to them. I understand the common struggles of losing a professional identity, giving up a second income, being isolated from the outside world and feeling lonely and overwhelmed. As I pray and encourage other moms, I let them know that I have been in their shoes, that they are not ruining their children's lives, and that God will help them parent their children just as He helped me. I am honest about my own struggles, I share the knowledge that I wish I would have been told earlier in my stay-at-home mom journey, and God passes some measure of comfort from me to others—all by His grace.

Although we are called to be compassionate and encouraging, I am not saying that we should condone or not call out sinful behavior. But, let's face it. We are all sinners. We as Christians assume everyone understands who God is and knows how much He loves us. People don't, however, understand God's loving nature because far too many times they see Christians, who are supposed to be God's representatives, acting like those who don't know Jesus. Sometimes we may think that we are above God's standards because He loves us. Sometimes we tend to overlook and justify our own sin. Then, when someone calls us out on

---

[33] John 3:16
[34] Isaiah 55:8-9

our sin, we may get defensive. If someone calls us out, consider what they are saying, and ask the Lord if they are correct. He will show you.

We are supposed to be a people of the "Book." We are supposed to be so well versed in every aspect of God's Word that we literally eat, breathe and sleep the knowledge that it affords. We are called to use God's profound knowledge and wisdom found in the Bible, not to condemn— but to share the hope of Christ that is found on its pages. Christ's love does not condemn, it invites people to a new way.[35]

What are some other ways we can share God's love with others? To answer this question we will need to rediscover God's character. Where should we start on our quest for rediscovery? How about at the beginning? Not just the beginning of our existence; but, let's start at the beginning of the Bible, when God created the first man and woman. Take a moment to imagine what it might have been like in the Garden of Eden. I'll give you a glimpse of what it was like. It started with LOVE.

Tying God's Apron Strings Around Your Heart

When you think of compassion what comes to your mind? Is it being broken hearted over someone else's circumstances, and then, allowing that brokenness to motivate you to act on that person's behalf? This resulting action may be as simple as a prayer lifted up to God asking Him to intervene. Or, it might be a moment of your time offered to help an elderly woman carry her groceries. It may even be an unplanned visit made to someone who is sick or sad. When was the last time you adjusted your plans to help another person whether you knew them or not? If it's been a while ask God to open your eyes to those around you who need compassion. Then show the love of Christ by responding in a tangible way.

---

[35] Hebrews 13:1; 1 Corinthians 13:1-13

Chapter 11
Giving

"I have shown you in every way, by laboring like this, that you must support the weak. And remember the words of the Lord Jesus, that He said, 'It is more blessed to give than to receive.' "
Acts 20:35, NKJV

In the Book of Genesis we read about the Garden of Eden, where an apron was first used for protection. *"And the eyes of them both were opened, and they knew that they were naked; and they sewed fig leaves together, and made themselves aprons" (Genesis 3:7, KJV)*. Since the beginning, God has given us abundant gifts, including the gift of protection through sacrifice. Receiving His bountiful gifts, considering how meticulously He cares for us, and seeing the incomprehensible sacrifice His Son endured for us helps show how to give sacrificially. These actions show us that not only His gifts—but also His sacrifice—are rooted in love.

Envision receiving the gift of a beautiful, tranquil garden. Large majestic trees are everywhere. Sunbeams shine through long dark branches that almost touch the earth. Birds lightly float in the sapphire hue of the heavens. A warm fragrant breeze sweeps across the land and beckons us to breathe deeply. All we need is before us. The abundance of color represented by the multitude of fruit is tantalizing to our eyes and taste buds. Vegetation and flora linger in every available space completing the Master's design. A magnificent flow of water can be heard as we pass the crystalline river where brilliant fish engage in playful activity. Exquisite creatures stroll along side us. Fear is not present because the creatures do not harm us. Our heart is at peace and all is right in the world.

Our Father God did indeed plant this garden as a gift for us. Every sense we possess is completely absorbed in the environment in which we stand. He loves us so much that nothing less than paradise will do as our dwelling. This love is the kind of love that God has for us. Paradise is where he wanted us to live. In paradise, no insects trouble us. The perfect temperature warms and cools our bodies and labor fulfills us. This scenario describes what God wanted for us. This life in paradise was His plan. This perfect place, this special home for humans, His most beloved creations was His loving gift.[36] We are so precious to Him that His perfect image was the only model that would suffice as a basis for humankind.[37]

In any relationship, the path of love must flow both ways for the relationship to be mutually beneficial. God began His journey with man by preparing a gorgeous garden for Him to share. This paradise was just the beginning of an unwavering stream of blessings that He would give for the sake of love. God calls us to pass on this love, because He wants us to love our neighbor as ourselves.[38] The greatest commandment ever given was to love your God with all your heart, soul, and mind.[39]

I wonder, though, if we are reciprocating the love that God has shown us. The Bible says, "Greater love hath no man than this, that a man lay down his life for his friends."[40] In the past when I read this passage, I always pictured someone literally jumping in front of a bullet. But I think God also means something deeper. I think he is asking us if we are we willing to die to our desires every day and live for Jesus so that others will also have hope? Are we willing to lay our life of comfort down for our friends? The sacrifice God desires would not be an impulse of the moment, but rather an act of ongoing godly obedience. It would compel us to give our life each day, every day, for as long as we have breath. This sacrifice entails not living for our own gain, or even the gain of Heaven, but for the gain of the lost. Are we willing to lay our life down that much, that often? If actions speak louder than words, what does the pattern of serving in our life say about our love for God and others? Does it say that I am laying my life down or does it say that I don't love others enough to sacrifice my time, abilities or resources?

Sacrificial giving is not easy but God's Apron will protect us from bitterness that can grow out of a sense of obligation. Sacrifice is an act of love, not obligation. God taught me this lesson about giving during the last ten years as I sacrificed my financial stability, my plans, my hopes, my comforts and my dreams for His plan. Because I had always enjoyed

---

[36] Genesis 2:8
[37] Genesis 1:26
[38] Matthew 19:19
[39] Matthew 22:37–38
[40] John 15:13, KJV

working outside the home, my husband and I both initially felt that I should keep working when we had children. But God made it clear that I was to stay home at least until they went to school. After my children were old enough to start preschool, I just knew I would go back to work. However, God then showed me it was His plan that I was to homeschool my children. I couldn't believe it. No one in my family had ever homeschooled their children. I barely knew anything about it. I posed every opposition to God's command (I'm not qualified, I can't afford it and what about socialization?). He told me after much deliberation on my part that I should do it. Why—well, because He told me to. Now that's blunt, isn't it! There was no mistaking His words.

I did as God commanded and I am so glad that I did. Just as staying home with my children as infants and toddlers brought sacrifice, homeschooling them through grade school is no different. I would not change it because my family can now focus on what God wants us to do each day, instead of adhering to a schedule that someone else believes is best. My love for God and my love for my family makes the sacrifice worth it because I want them to also know and love God. He has also given me new dreams, new hopes and He has taken care of us financially. My focus is no longer on my sacrifice as it was years ago. My focus is only on the future destination of my soul and the souls of my family members. We look forward to eternity in Heaven, with our Father who loved us so much that He was willing to first sacrifice His son, who died on a cross for us.

As I raise my children, God cultivates my ability to give to them by offering me His Apron to put on each time I feel like giving up. He offered me his love first through His sacrifice, and then by giving me prayer, His Word and His Church.

After my experience giving up much of myself for my family, I am here to tell you that accepting His sacrifice and putting on God's Apron not only equips us to lovingly sacrifice our desires for His, but it also sets the stage for us to patiently share His love with others. By tasting His goodness, sampling His abundant recipe for our lives, and experiencing His promises in the Bible, we are compelled to let His love overflow out of ourselves into the lives of those who don't yet know Him. After all, someone made a sacrifice to invite you to the table and share God's Apron with you or you would not be where you are today. So be obedient and pass on His love. You can carry a portion of God's love and give it away. The world needs it.

Tying God's Apron Strings Around Your Heart

Are you fighting a sacrifice God is calling you to make for your good and His glory? If so, I encourage you to pray that God would change your heart or change your circumstance to align with His plans. Ask Him to show you exactly what He is asking of you. He may likely only reveal a step at a time. But, you will be blessed and learn more at each step of obedience. Also, recall what God has given you since you have been following Him and be grateful. Gratitude cultivates a giving heart. When you consider what He has done, it will make your sacrifice seem small in comparison. If you have just recently placed your trust in Jesus, thank him for everything good in your life. Start with thanking Him for breath, for friends and anything else you can think of.

Chapter 12
Church

And let us consider one another in order to stir up love and good works, not forsaking the assembling of ourselves together, as is the manner of some, but exhorting one another, and so much the more as you see the Day approaching.
Hebrews 10:24-25, NKJV

I recently had an opportunity to talk to a man while I was waiting at a local place of business. He knew my husband was a minister and he asked me where Kenny was preaching. After hearing my reply, he began to casually inform me that he attends many different churches. Because of his initial question about attending our church, I knew he was considering attending yet another church. I then asked if he was having trouble finding somewhere he felt comfortable. Unlike some people I talk to, his main complaint about local churches didn't center around feeling accepted; his complaint was the length of time church was in session. More to the point, he was irritated with what he perceived as long-winded preachers.

When I asked if he felt that he was limiting the amount of time God should take to speak to a person's heart, his reply took me quite by surprise. He said something to this effect, "They should be able to get the point in a shorter amount of time. If they don't, preaching longer only causes everyone to lose interest." I was thankful for his candor. I appreciate honesty.

So many times in the South, everyone feels things should be sugar coated from our conversations right down to the vegetables on our dinner table. This sugar coating leaves many of us wondering where we actually stand and where the truth really lays. But, as my conversation with this man continued, God reminded me that our hearts are often hard and stubborn. The preacher might be able to spend less time on the subject if people were more prone to receive all of his words and adjust

69

their lives to reflect the truth those words imparted. A preacher is held accountable by God for what he preaches or teaches to the congregation.[41] He must be guided by the Holy Spirit about his subject matter and time management. Because God is the only one who knows the heart, we must be careful not to assume the preacher is long-winded. Rather, we should remind ourselves that God has given the pastor, His servant, a message to share with the congregation. The length and topic of a pastor's message or teaching is based on God's leading.[42] Perhaps the question we should be asking as we sit in church each week is, "Do I want to hear what God has chosen to say today?" I believe, most often, that God will show us that our job is to listen and respond in obedience. Yes, we are to check what the pastor preaches against Scripture, but we are not to doubt his methods because they don't fit into a "quick fix" mold that our culture is most accustomed to.

The more I pondered this man's concern in my heart, the more I felt sadness for him. He claimed a tie to Jesus by claiming a church affiliation. However, he couldn't even decide which church that should be. He apparently did not have a strong connection to any of the churches he mentioned, nor did He seem to attend church for the sake of hearing from God. The way the words rolled off his tongue revealed his view that he thought others must be lacking in understanding. But, it was obvious to me that he truly didn't understand why God tells us to attend church. It was also clear that he didn't know what a vibrant relationship to God really means. To him church attendance is—as many seem to think—an obligation begrudgingly met. He feels that his complaints are warranted if the amount of preaching time exceeds the time that he is comfortable listening.

I wondered when he had last felt God speak directly to him—or if he ever had. I reminded him that even if he limited his time with God, God would still make time for him. God still loved him; If there was a relationship there, it was so distant I could scarcely recognize it. If he had not told me, I would never have known that he knew Jesus. What saddened me the most was that this man didn't seem to know that his words and actions gave off the impression that he didn't know Jesus. He feels safe from God's judgment because of his church membership and sparse attendance. But, I wonder how safe he really is. I wonder if He is truly saved. His fruit seemed withered. His relationship with God seemed

41 Hebrews 13:17; James 3:1; Acts 20:28
42 Colossians 1:25-28; Malachi 2:7; Jerimiah 3:15

distant. I am afraid for him—just like I am afraid for all people who may end up in Hell.

Church attendance does not save us. A relationship to God through Jesus Christ is the only way to be saved.[43] We attend church because we love God. We want to be near Him and in fellowship with others who also love Him. We want to set aside time each week to worship Him and thank Him for what He has done for us. It is our reasonable service. Our attitude about church is a reflection of our relationship with God. It was not man who decided we needed church.[44] It was God.

In Thom Rainer's book, *The Autopsy of a Deceased Church,* one of the reasons he lists for the death of a local body of believers is that the members are in denial. They don't seem to see the obvious from the outside looking in: the church is malnourished. The members slowly become more isolated and inward focused rather than loving the outside world. Many times they start to nest with new paint, new windows and new carpet in the church building. What the congregation really needs instead is a revitalized heart dedicated to God. I think the same need for a heart change exists for many individuals. I have no other way to explain the exorbitant amount of people that I encounter on a regular basis that claim Jesus but they live as if they don't know him.

People are looking to us—His people—to see if we live out what we say we believe. Based on the fruit and peace in our lives, people who live outside of our churches will decide if they want to taste Jesus for themselves. I wonder how much our relationship with God really matters to us, because it seems many are willing to compromise what we say or believe about His Truth. We alter our stance or withhold the truth to receive acceptance from the world that doesn't know Him. As Christians, by not standing our ground on unpopular biblical truths, we are failing our country and our community. We are failing to answer God's command to live our life differently.[45] We are to live by His rules if we claim to be His. I have heard many say, "What's this world coming to?" The darkness is growing because we do not share the light of Jesus Christ in spite of the darkness. In other words, we are not living the way He wants us to, and we aren't committed to telling others about Him. What we have been given—what Christ suffered and died for—we hide for the sake of being comfortable. We place our own comfort and the

---

[43] John 14:6
[44] Hebrews 10:24–25
[45] 1 Peter 2:1–10

comfort of others in our congregation above the need to save a lost world.

How comfortable do we think it will be in Hell? Hell won't last just a short while like the man I met wanted a sermon to be. Hell lasts forever. Do we hate our neighbors so much that we want to freely let them believe a lie about their salvation only for them to discover that they were wrong when it is too late? If we let them think that they are safely protected from Hell if we don't clearly know if Jesus is Lord and Savior of their lives, we are doing them an eternal disservice. We are also absolving ourselves of the responsibility that comes from the freedom we have been given in Christ. By not telling others more about Him, we are ourselves disobeying Him.

I see a very large deficit in our spiritual diet today. It is the undedicated attitude many have about church. The lackadaisical way we handle the amazing gift of a God-centered church is causing a huge gap in our relationship with God. Not understanding the role of the church in our lives can cause our spiritual health to hang in the balance. If we have children, the adverse effect on our family's spiritual health is even more grave. We are teaching our children that church isn't important. Christ died to establish His Church. If the Church as a whole is worth Christ's life, it is worth our time.

Sports, even those played on Saturday can hinder Sunday morning worship because we become too tired and worn out to pay attention to what God may be saying to us. We make plans for Sunday that don't include God. We don't love Him enough to allow time for Him—not even on Sunday, which is supposed to be a Holy Day for Christians, is set aside for Him. We don't love others enough to come to church and learn so that we may teach them what we have learned about God's love and Jesus sacrifice. I pray that God help us to love so much that we are metaphorically holding the ankles of those who are deceived and blindly headed into Hell. If they want to go, let us at least use everything within us to divert their plans. And, if in the end they succeed, we can know in our hearts we were willing to sacrifice everything for their well-being.

Just like the man I was blessed to talk with, we need to understand why we claim Jesus and know what that really means. We need to take a hard look in the mirror and ask, "Do others see Jesus in me?" If we can't see Him, neither will they. We need to see church for what it is: a lifeline to a closer relationship to God. Church is a weekly nutritional booster shot that helps us live out our faith every day. In a world where the mention of God's name can evoke wrath and disapproval, it is more important than ever for Christians to assemble among like-minded, God desiring individuals. These like-minded people in our churches need to be willing to encourage and pray us through the turmoil raging outside our church doors. God has a Word for us. If we won't meet Him at His appointed time and place, we could miss that life-giving Word. We could miss the protection our Apron is trying to give us. We could miss the opportunity to be strengthened which enables us to share the Apron with others. God doesn't waste words. If He has put words on our pastor's heart, it will be crucial to our spiritual nutrition. Therefore, we must make sure we are getting a properly balanced meal. This well-rounded meal includes our pastor's words—the main course of our spiritual nutrition— and the sides of support and accountability from a healthy church community. As a new stay at home mom years ago, I had a longing in my soul and I began to search for a church to call home. I had attended several different churches, but finally decided to return to the church of my youth. One Wednesday evening when the pastor gave an invitation for the people of the congregation to recommit their lives to Christ, I felt God tugging at my heart. I went forward in obedience. Shortly after that night, God placed a deep hunger in my soul for knowledge of His Word. I began to attend every class, service and pot luck meal that was available. I remember taking pages of notes and rereading them when I got home because I wanted so desperately to be closer to God.

I was welcomed with open arms by the community in that church. They were willing to pray for me anytime day or night. They were interested in seeing me through whatever God had planned. They encouraged me when I needed it. God had taught me what a godly church family looks like during those years. No one was perfect, but many were dedicated to God. The model God showed me though this church family is the one I still prayerfully follow today as my family ministers to others at the church where God has planted us. God allows me to pour into others today the same way He allowed others to pour into me nearly a decade ago.

To be fully covered by God's Apron, we must heed our pastor's teaching, and we must be in community with other believers at church. We are called to be members of the Body of Christ. We cannot effectively tie His Apron strings alone nor can we ensure that we don't take off the Apron when we are tempted or going through hardship without the Body of Christ. Let's be part of this Holy Body, and let's help each other keep the Apron on.

Tying God's Apron Strings Around Your Heart

Are you regularly attending church? I'm not talking about listening to a preacher on TV or online! Have you made a commitment to serve God in the church where you regularly attend? If not, I pray you start today. Ask God to show you where and how He would have you serve Him for the glory of His Kingdom. And next time you feel a little disgruntled about how long someone teaches or preaches, ask God to open your heart to receive all the spiritual nutrition He wants to give even if it takes a little longer than you are accustomed to.

Chapter 13
God's Voice

"My sheep hear My voice, and I know them, and they follow Me. And I give them eternal life, and they shall never perish; neither shall anyone snatch them out of My hand."
John 10:27-28, NKJV

I look out across my foggy lawn. A cloud of mist blankets my surroundings hushing the outside world from my serene sanctuary. Barely a chirp of a lovely bird transcends the stillness. The earth is completely saturated by moistness and I feel the crispness in the air as I inhale the freshness from an open window. I relish in the moment and thank God for the peace that seems abundant during the dawn of this tranquil morning. No one is stirring in the house. My children are still warm in their beds and hopefully dreaming of childhood fancies. My husband has departed for quite another world. He is headed to a more difficult environment dictated by a pecking order of hectic schedules and periodic conflict. We thank God for our land and a home, but these commitments bring pressure to his existence. I see the weariness on his face. Even in the peace of such a rare moment, I know that elsewhere in the world, turmoil, war, hate and oppression rule the day. Many are suffering throughout the world. Maybe the pain faced is caused by the hand of an abuser or by decay of a mortal body. Causes of turmoil may vary, but be assured, many are suffering.

My thoughts are drawn to those facing the depths of desperation. I wonder if they know our God, who is the true source of consolation. I realize that to be comforted by God, we have to pause long enough to hear His voice. We have to believe that He exists and is willing to help us. We might even have to put aside our schedule, our five-year plan or even our pride to hear Him. We have to stop long enough to listen. But often, we are too addicted to our activity. Our thought processes are too programed on the loud station that this world transmits. Sometimes it seems as if we can't step outside the mundane, redundant circle to put ourselves in a position to hear God—even for a season. So the hustle and the bustle continues stealing a little more of our energy every day until one day, the pressure builds and we break. Maybe we are going through a divorce or we impulsively quit a job. But something propels us to a new phase in our lives. We need an escape. We want to feel alive. We are tired of being weary. We keep changing our hair, buying new clothes, positioning ourselves to earn more money. No matter what we do, we feel as Solomon did when he wrote, "All is vanity." [46]

Only so many hours exist in a day. Once the hours are gone, we will not get them back. So, why do we spend so much of our lives doing mundane, menial tasks? I am not talking about gainful employment. I am talking about the other things we do to keep ourselves occupied. I too suffer from the malady of making myself overly busy with non-eternally focused activity. So His finger points first in my direction. Cleaning tasks do carry some weight for our health and well-being. Just thinking of them now brings an urgency to my mind and grief to my heart bidding me to leave this task of writing that God has bestowed upon me. Some part of me thinks I should race frantically until every last detail is attended to.

Not this morning, though. It all can wait. I want to sit at the Master's feet. I want to step into the presence of God by praying and spending time reading my Bible. Every day is important. But today is even more so because my heart is troubled by issues God has allowed me to see. I am grieved because so many others seem blinded to them. This hectic race we are running does not lead to God's Kingdom! And, the one who dies with the most toys certainly does not win! *So how do we get to where we need to be?* That's simple. We get there by our position.[47] As we are still, we can position ourselves with open hearts to hear God's voice and see the matters on His heart that were not in our view when we were traveling at the speed of this world.

I am brought to this understanding today because I need to hear it today. You see, I fear deeply and inwardly what the future holds for my family and my country. We are in the danger zone; yet, we live as if we control the universe. God alone has this task well in hand and lovingly reminds us there is nothing He can't handle. He tells us that there are no depths to which He will not go to redeem us.[48] He literally holds our lives

---

[46] Ecclesiastes 1:2–3
[47] Psalm 46:10
[48] Mark 10:27; Ephesians 1:3-10

in His hands. So why is He the last person we go to in times of trouble? Why is His Word, the Bible, often the last place we go for answers? Our relationship with Him is strained or non-existent because we are often not living with our focus on God's plans for the day.

Between regretting the past and experiencing anxiety about the future, we rarely live in the present. It is no wonder we can't hear God's voice when He speaks to us. Our minds are not tuned into the "present" station. God speaks in the present tense. He speaks in the here and now. If our mind is not focused where He is, we could miss hearing His important words. *How do we know that God is speaking?* His Word tells us that He is. It also tells us that we hear His voice. If we, can hear His voice, then He must be speaking.[49]

Life is so much more joyful when we live it with our focus on today. We want to rush through the journey. What is happening today will never happen again. We need to take time to enjoy it. God's Word says there is no guarantee of tomorrow.[50] If we lived everyday as if it were our last, would that perspective change our actions? Would we linger a little longer with our friends or family? Would we relish the taste of our favorite food? Would we pause to gaze upon the wonders of this world, a snow capped mountain, a sleeping baby or the smell of fragrance in the air? I think we would. But, we are so caught up in our to-do list; we can't see past it. We are running from place to place in a mad rush. It is no wonder God tells us to be still and know that I am God.[51] If we are never still or quiet, it is nearly impossible to hear his voice. This frantic pace is all the more reason to take intentional measures to position ourselves with openness and awareness to enable us to hear His voice.

Our stillness is vital to our spiritual nutrition. It is time we slowed down long enough to digest what God is placing before us. Can you taste it? Can you smell it? Do you feel your strength growing? Do you see everything else fading until at last you are one with the Father? Put on your Apron, share a meal with your Father and let yourself be nourished by His presence. As you commune with Him, let the pressures of this world disappear in comparison to the vastness of the God of the universe.

---

[49] John 10:27
[50] James 4:14
[51] Psalm 46:10

Tying God's Apron Strings Around Your Heart

Do you take time each day to be still with God? Do you write down what He does or says in that time? If you don't make this practice a regular habit, I encourage you to start or recommit to doing so today. I know that some days it seems impossible and that other days you won't feel like it. Those days are likely the times you will need it the most. Make a commitment now. Start with 15 minutes with the intention of letting the time increase after a while. God wants to visit with you today. Please don't miss this amazing opportunity!

Chapter 14
Prayer

And pray in the Spirit on all occasions with all kinds of prayers and requests. With this in mind, be alert and always keep on praying for all the Lord's people.
Ephesians 6:18, NIV

A gathering around the dinner table is nothing new. We try to gather around ours at least once a day. Granted, I usually have to clear off everything from baseball gloves to this week's mail. Occasionally, I have to even move a sock or sneaker that for whatever reason has found its way to the kitchen table. We experience excitement as we prepare the meal with many little hands involved. We relax, laugh and discuss the day's activities, much of which leave us with tears of joy. We gather in the middle of the room, chairs retrieved from every available space as we rest side by side waiting for "The Blessing." Volunteers are requested and little hands shoot up all around the table. I love their eagerness. The food is cold by the time all the "thank yous" and the "help the sick puppies" are lifted up to God. Not that I mind. These children are learning that prayer starts with just a little talk with Jesus. No one who is eager to pray is denied the opportunity. I have learned to keep the food warm in the oven until the very last minute and place all the food in containers with lids to help keep it warm as we remember to thank the One who has given everything for us. I don't want to cut our prayer time short. I hope it teaches us to take time to be thankful and to slow down long enough to enjoy life.

It hasn't been very long since my oldest grandson was visiting and became one of these prayer warriors. His eyes were tightly closed underneath his small rimmed glasses. He swayed his head back and forth, raised his eyebrows and moved his hands in expression as he talked never once opening his eyes. He thanked God for the wonderful day and the baby chicks that hatched during the week. When he thanked God for the food, he listed every dish by name: green beans, mashed potatoes, steak, salad, water, milk and cornbread. I noticed he left off the broccoli, probably because as he would put it, "It's not my favorite." Every now and then, he paused fooling us all into thinking he was finished only to discover that he was eager to share with the Lord just a little more. He then turned his thoughts to others as he asked God to help the old folks in the nursing home who "can't get up good." He also prayed for anyone crossing the street, because we know how scary that can be. What a sweet heart he has! He already understands who the Giver and Protector is for every last person on this planet. He knows that prayer isn't something rehearsed, but that prayer is an act of communication fostering an age old relationship between man and his Creator. If asked, my grandson would not be able to put it in such adult terms, but nevertheless, he believes that his prayers are heard and answered by our Father in Heaven.

Prayer—talking to God—seems simple. But, for some reason, it can appear to be difficult. Maybe, it's how we look at it. It is not a "sit on Santa's knee talk" and give God a list of what we think we need. True prayer is simply communicating with a loving Father. It's like sharing a cup of coffee between friends. It's all about the relationship. We talk about our concerns, thank Him for our blessings and leave our baggage at His feet. We trust Him to control and rule the universe as only He can. We rest in His presence. We soak in the sunshine of His countenance. We wait as His Holy Spirit within us has a family reunion with His Counterparts: God, the Father and Jesus, His Son. We let the struggle of this world fade as we worship the One worthy of all praise. Maybe we sing a song or have a melody in our heart as we catch a glimpse of eternity in the arms of our Father. Then we open our Bible, longing for a revelation from Him. His Words before us are something tangible we can touch, see and smell. The binding is worn, the pages wrinkled and the once new smell of leather is far removed. Like an old friend, we can't let go of this book and its Words because of the support they bring and the miles of life they have seen us through. The pages prove their trustworthiness. It's life altering as we ask God to look within our soul and reveal places that we ourselves don't even want to go.

Prayer shouldn't be cold and calculated. It isn't all about me. It is about knowing the source of the power. Prayer isn't only reactive, but it is also proactive. We are to pray without ceasing.[52] Maybe we are physically unable to do that—or so we think. But, God wants us to

---

[52] 1 Thessalonians 5:17

continually be in contact with Him, drawing from His unending strength and loving nature.

I've learned about the power of prayer and how God gives strength and love in ways I never thought possible. The story of my grandchild praying touches my heart, as my prayers touch the heart of God. Just as I delight in hearing my grandchildren pray, God also delights in hearing me pray. And, just as God answers my grandson's prayers, He answers mine—including the life-changing, I-can't-fix-this-myself prayer.

For my husband and me, this type of life changing prayer started with changing our business and completely rearranging the source of our income. You see, we owned a video business. It had been my parents' business until they separated. My husband and I had purchased it from them, and I quit my job to manage the store. I loved people and movies, so the business seemed like a grand adventure to me at first. However, after a few years, as God began to draw me into a closer relationship with Him, He began to show me how much movie content was extremely ungodly. The more I studied the Bible, the clearer God's voice became. I began to feel guilty about profiting off the sinful messages that many movies contain. I felt God saying, "Sell your business and stay home with your children." What? How was I going to support my family without an income? Could this really be God's plan?

Through prayer and circumstances, God made His will known. I was supposed to sell the business. I know everyone thought I was crazy. But, there was no doubt in my mind. God began to press His truth upon my heart so strongly that I wanted to obey if only to have relief from the burden I felt.

Looking back, I realize that when I first heard God say that I was to sell the business, I would not surrender. That's why God kept pressing. I remember the overwhelming relief as I sacrificed my livelihood and professional identity and laid them down at God's feet. I can't explain how that happened other than through God's mercy and grace. Because even though I didn't know the outcome, I had complete peace about the situation. I did not even profit from the inventory liquidation. I sold everything as cheaply as possible. I just wanted this chapter in my life closed, and I didn't feel God wanted me to profit from the sale.

The sale left my husband and I with about $100,000.00 in business debt because the business carried a mortgage. I felt God had just closed the door on the only way I thought the business could turn a profit—by staying in business. We then cashed in my husband's retirement to pay off personal debt to offset the decrease in household income. We refinanced our personal mortgage even though we only had nine years left on the note.

Through all this financial rearranging it felt like we were starting back at ground zero. Those were tumultuous times. But, though it all, God continued to grow me spiritually, He asked me to trust Him more, and He showed me more of His amazing love.

During this time of rebuilding, an even greater prayer was answered: my husband accepted Jesus Christ as His Savior and became a Christian. On the Wednesday evening (at church) when He was saved, no one had a dry eye as we all witnessed the long awaited answer to our prayers! We were no longer unequally yoked.

My husband, with his new found peace in Jesus, would see that God's answer to prayer would not end with his salvation. The following year as we began to prepare our taxes, a new situation arose. When I met with the accountant, He informed me that we would need to take a second mortgage on our home to pay for the taxes owed on the retirement withdrawal.

I was devastated at the news that once again seemed to leave our finances at risk. When my husband came home from work and heard the news, he quietly went to a separate room and closed the door. In a few minutes the phone rang. It was the accountant. He was calling after hours because he had some additional news that would lift my burden—and he didn't want me to be upset any longer than necessary. After reviewing our finances, he could see we had taken an enormous loss in closing our business. This loss would offset the money he originally thought we would owe. In fact, we were instead going to receive a refund!

I thanked the accountant for his kindness in calling as soon as he knew and ran immediately to my husband. When I opened the door that separated us, I found my husband in prayer. He looked up at me upon hearing the news. With tears in both our eyes, my husband said, "I have been in prayer surrendering my will and asking God to handle the situation however He chooses." We both began to cry and thank God for His deliverance and mercy in letting us know His plan sooner rather than later.

God's mercy and timing is always perfect. It never occurred to us to close the business the same year that we withdrew the retirement funds. But, God knew the timing was critical to our financial survival. It is no wonder He pressed me so, time was running out, and I, with my human limitations, didn't even know it. We had prayed, obeyed God and prayed some more. The circumstances weren't easy, but the results were definitely for our good and for His glory. Not only did He take care of our finances, but He drew my husband to Himself, and drew another soul to His Kingdom. Today, my husband is a pastor, committing his life to sharing the love he found in Jesus to whomever God brings to our church. You never know what God is going to do with prayer—or how much it may change your life.

Without the vital nutrient of prayer in our lives, we will always be spiritually malnourished when difficult financial, professional or relational challenges arise. We may even starve ourselves and become spiritually anorexic. We need both the church, our booster shot, and prayer, our immunity support system. Without prayer, we will definitely succumb to sickness with the cold circumstances of life. Then, our sickness will cause us to be too weak to even know that we have caught the world's virus. Let's protect ourselves and use prayer to tie the Apron around our necks and waists so that when difficult struggles arise, our protection is already in place. This protection will allow us to focus on God's ability instead of our own overwhelming circumstances.

Tying God's Apron Strings Around Your Heart

Can you remember a time that an answered prayer changed your life? Recall it and thank God for it. If you are struggling today, lift up a special prayer, being as honest and specific as a child would. God delights in hearing from you!

Chapter 15
Stillness

Then He said, "Go out, and stand on the mountain before the LORD." And behold, the LORD passed by, and a great and strong wind tore into the mountains and broke the rocks in pieces before the LORD, but the LORD was not in the wind; and after the wind an earthquake, but the LORD was not in the earthquake; and after the earthquake a fire, but the LORD was not in the fire; and after the fire a still small voice.
1 Kings 19:11-12, NKJV

My car rolls to a stop as the man with his hard hat, work boots and luminous vest turns his red octagon shaped sign from slow to stop. I can see in my rear view mirror a line of cars slowly and intermittently forming in a snake like manner around the curve and length is added to it with each new vehicle.

I was making a short trip to a town near our home with my grandchildren when I was given the hand signal to stop. At first, there was much excitement to keep my young passengers occupied. Dump trucks are rushing by; each one is emptying a load of gravel leaving an enormous billowing cloud of dust behind. A blue tractor travels at a much slower pace and the rider reaches down to the street and places the orange cones that keep us all at a safe distance. The youngest boy in my car, then four years old, yells in his very outdoor voice, "Oh Gosh, he could fall out. It gots no sides on it!" The tractor travels along the road beside us passing each car until it disappears altogether.

To everyone's dismay, our life-sized construction display is short lived and about seven minutes into our layover, the grumbling of the children begins. "May we get out of our car seat?" they ask in unison behind me. I can hear the clicking of seat belts releasing before I even give a reply. Immediately I retort with a stern, "Put your seat belt back on! We won't be here that long." I must admit, I too was wishing this boredom would end. As bodies shuffled, whines multiplied. Little frames slumped over like deflated balloons within their confined spaces.

I couldn't help but chuckle just a little because the display was much more dramatized than the circumstances warranted, but you can't reason with four-year-old boys! Their reactions were over inflated as they expressed their suffering in the air-conditioned car strapped to a seat. They acted as if they were infested by bugs.

In actuality, we were only delayed about ten minutes. It seemed longer, especially with the atmosphere projected from the rear. When the much anticipated release came, I could hear small voices in deep conversation recalling what must have been a double traffic jam. They wondered if the town we were going to visit was bigger than the one we live in, and if it brought about delays of this nature, no one ever wanted to visit this town again.

I am sure this familiar scene has all too often played out in mothers' taxis as they haul children all over America. But it got me to thinking—dangerous I know—about how we, as children of God, act very much the same way. When our loving Father tells us to wait, we squirm, we whine and we think that we will literally die. We plead with God, "Anything but waiting. I can't take it. Please don't make me."

Just like my grandchildren forming their opinions of what must have happened, we don't always understand the reason behind God's plan. He may simply know we need the rest. Just like He taught me the importance of rest with my anxiety attacks, He may bring about circumstances to make us learn this lesson if we do not learn to wait. Everything is in His timing as He orchestrates and aligns all the circumstances to allow for His purposes to be completed. He knows we have gotten too busy doing too much "good" and that we have forgotten why we should be motivated to do "good" in the first place.

Scripture says, "Be still and know that I am God." [53] Be still, be quiet—just plain be. It is hard. We will have to stop reacting and stop thinking long enough to just dwell in the presence of God. We need to feel the warmth and calm that penetrates our busy existence. This stillness keeps us grounded where we need to be. It keeps us close to God.

I have seen rods placed in the earth and attached to wires running up to the rooftop of homes in the South. These rods deflect lightning and help ensure the safety of people inside. They help houses and the people in them stay rooted, if you will.

[53] Psalm 46:10

86

Spending time with God in complete surrender of our will, being still, affords us the same type of protection as lightning rods do. God's Apron takes the energy and circumstances thrust upon us and deflects them to the place where they can take the blow—in Him. We are not simply doing nothing. We are choosing to place a spiritual rod over our minds and our households to prepare ourselves for potential storms. So next time the world around us, traveling at the speed of lightning, is more than we can handle, step into the presence of the Lord. Don't speak. Just be. The Bible says, "Be still and know." To truly know Him, we must first be still.

Tying God's Apron Strings Around Your Heart
When was the last time God forced you to be still by making you wait? How did you handle that? Sometimes God's delays enable Him to breathe into your life by speaking His message to you. Do you have a tendency to be impatient during these "waiting times?" If so, ask God to help you accept them gratefully. He is enabling you to receive the time of rest you need to travel on your spiritual journey more faithfully.

Chapter 16
Die

"I have been crucified with Christ; it is no longer I who live, but Christ lives in me; and the life which I now live in the flesh I live by faith in the Son of God, who loved me and gave Himself for me."
Galatians 2:20, NKJV

I can feel my muscles tense as my mind is searching to understand the real issue underneath the rant being displayed before me. The woman engaged with such emotion seems to offer only vague points for some unknown reason. I am unable to grasp what causes her to object to my conversation. I stated that God does not approve of a sexual relationship outside of a biblical marriage.[54] Although she is a third party not directly involved in the conversation, she seems certain of her own understanding. She is bent on convincing me of her rightness. In a very debate-like manner, with strength in her voice and an obvious lack of compassion for the feelings of others, she restates that she was offended. I find it quite curious that one who openly admits that she doesn't care what others think about what she says is causing a scene as a result of what has been spoken neither to nor about her. The subject matter has evidently hit a nerve, and she cannot let it be. As time runs out and I must go, she hands me her card and says she really feels we should discuss this more. In other words, since I am obviously not yet persuaded to her way of thinking, she wants more time to help me see the light—her light—because no view but hers could be correct.

After I arrived at home, I took a brief moment to examine the card and lay it on my bedside table. My intentions were to keep her at the front of my prayer list. But, as I prayed, I felt God say, "Throw the card away. This fight is not yours. It is Mine." I knew in my heart that He was

---

54 Hebrews 13:4; 1 Corinthians 7:1–2, 8–9

removing any future temptation I might feel to state my case, so to speak. You see, He had already done that. He had stated His case as I was sharing my experience with another. This lady had overheard part of a conversation and intervened. Her reaction proved His point. I had been obedient and my task was done. To do more would be sinful because it wasn't God's plan. I was to let it be and walk away.

I understand this strong-willed woman because I am like her sometimes. But I would not credit it to my gender or faith. Because sometimes when my will is strong, I am suffocating God's breath in a situation. His will is the only one that matters for the Christian woman. It doesn't matter if I am right. What matters is what God wants. For a strong-willed Southern woman, only the power of God could enable me to follow the command to discard her information. God might have more for me to do on another day; but today, I was to lay down the gauntlet and pick up the cross.[55] For today, the cross would be my silence.

Dying to self or dying to being right is hard for those of us with strong convictions. This willful death goes against our overwhelmingly strong desire to influence others as a result of our beliefs. We live full force like a hurricane for what we believe to be right. But, life is not a debate. Likewise, sharing our faith should not be combative. We must approach others as we do the throne of God, with humility and a desire to love above all. This kind of faith will take sacrifice and will most certainly leave us in a puddle of tears on a regular basis; our hearts will be broken over what God has allowed us to see that others can not. We know and see that many are blinded.

Thinking back to the incident with this lady, I realized that she talked much about how God is the only One who can open the eyes of understanding for those who cannot see clearly beyond their own experiences. This portion of her position was true; however, we can not use God's role as an excuse to absolve ourselves of the responsibility for what God tells us to do. He wants us to be involved in His work. We are not able to do anything of Kingdom value on our own. God is the one working, He is just allowing us to know Him better by experience, through obedience and because of time spent with Him. It is His work. We are just blessed to be a part of it. Many times He may use us to open the eyes of another. He may want us to speak words they need to hear. Much of the time, they may not like hearing the words that God has placed on our hearts to share.

---

[55] Matthew 16:24

As she continued to try to make her point, my mind stopped focusing on her words and more on the source of her disagreement. I wondered about the root—or rather the force—that drove her to make these statements. I cannot read a person's heart. But, I can see the actions that the secrets of a heart show to the outside world. As I watched her actions, I felt like I was watching a scene playing out in a movie. I was witnessing a dramatic moment where the storyline comes together and reveals something deeper.

I prayed—in an instant and in the Spirit—asking God to help me see beyond what felt like an attack from Satan himself. God would not want me to react based on pride, ownership or insult. I would need His strength. The rant had gone on long enough that I was becoming weary; I was afraid I would say something I shouldn't. I can definitely say God was gracious. Even though I felt offended, I did not feel the urge to defend myself. Nor did I feel the inclination to rise to the debate.

Within my soul, I could hear God speaking His words of encouragement to my heart. They sounded something like this, "I have pricked her heart because I wanted to open her eyes to something she is holding back from Me." He went on to say, "You knew the words placed on your heart—even the ones I told you to write—would sometimes offend people. I have prepared you to endure this uncomfortable scene—loud and messy, with others staring—just as I equipped you to write." God's Words were a soothing balm, a song, that played in my heart reminding me that I was—at least in that instant of time—in the center of God's will.

Later that night, in the darkness of my bedroom, I sat in the silence and asked God to search my heart and reveal any offense He might have against me. He didn't reveal anything else that evening although He often does. I also earnestly prayed for that lady on that particular evening asking God to bless her and to help me to hold no malice against her. I do not look forward to future encounters like this one. But I can rest assured that God will be with me when such encounters come.

As for the woman I encountered that day, God would later reveal her offense and the root from which it sprang. It seemed so simple, although anything from God is profound. I understood her better. I knew God would guide her, if she would allow it. Why did He reveal her motives to me? So that I could pray for her. Prayer is a powerful thing. In this case, God knew she would need prayers to overcome what He had planned, and I would need to pray as an act of humility and obedience allowing Him to continue the work that He had set before me. We are all a work in progress. We need to react less and pray more when offenses come our way. God can use a disagreement to strengthen both parties for His glory. But, we will have to die to self and die to being right. And that's not easy in this world driven by "my right" to do whatever I choose. But a child of God has no independent, earthly rights. We have something better. You see, we are bought and paid for by the blood of Jesus Christ.[56] It is not our life we are called to live any longer, but we are invited to live the life He desires for us. We are not slaves, but heirs.[57] We are his children. We bear His Name: the Name above all Names. And, as His children who have accepted Him, we belong to Him. He does not force us to love Him because love does not force. But, if we have chosen to accept His grace, we are saying I will die to self because Jesus now lives and I am dead.[58] When we die to self, it is not our flesh who lives, but Christ who lives in us.

Next time we encounter a less than desirable situation, we should pray before we speak, put on God's Apron, which sees our enemies through Christ's love and blood. This shield over our hearts enables us to decide to love instead of deciding to hate. And most of all, we should want to do the will of God by dying to what we want—even if we know we are right. If being right doesn't glorify God, then it is not useful to His Kingdom.

Tying God's Apron Strings Around Your Heart

Do you find it offensive when someone doesn't agree with you? Does a disagreement motivate you to prove how right you are? The next time you have a confrontational encounter, ask God to use you as a vessel for His love instead of allowing yourself to be drawn into a debate. I know that God will be faithful and you will be blessed in the process.

---

[56] 1 Corinthians 6:19–20
[57] Romans 8:16–17
[58] Galatians 2:20

Chapter 17
Reality Check

But the day of the Lord will come as a thief in the night, in which the heavens will pass away with a great noise, and the elements will melt with fervent heat; both the earth and the works that are in it will be burned up.
2 Peter 3:10, NKJV

In the movie Jane Eyre, a religious leader asks a young Jane how she can escape Hell. Jane, who states that Hell is a pit of fire, answers boldly: "Live well and not die, sir."

I wonder how many of us would admit that we tend to live life as if Jane's words in the classic movie were actually possible. We prefer to live as if we can escape death; many also avoid discussing death much of the time. But, unless Jesus returns before we die, death is the inevitable path for all of us. Instead of acting like death doesn't exist, we should come to grips with the future of our earthly bodies in a way that brings God the most glory.

According to a news story released in the last quarter of 2014, life expectancy in America has increased to 78.8 years. This may seem like a long time, but placed on a timeline beginning—well, at the beginning—and ending—you guessed it—with the end of time, our time spent on this planet is barely noticeable. It would barely warrant a pause. It would take up less space than one of the commas on this page. So, why do we tend to think we are so important? If we buy into the theory of evolution, human life isn't even sacred. After all, this theory suggests we came from nothing and transformed our way to where we are now.

Even if we don't agree with how the world was created, many do agree that it will not last forever. The Bible is clear in its account that God does plan to destroy this planet that we call home.[59] What value does that give to all the possessions that we are working each day to

---

[59] 2 Peter 3:10

accumulate? We will not be able to take anything from earth with us when we die. Stockpiling possessions will only, in most cases leave a pile of rubbish or worn out items for the next generation. This trash then contaminates our land, which is land that we don't even really own. Shortly after we die, another will purchase it and labor until they too meet the doors of death or possibly the devastation of bankruptcy.

We are not valuable, we are not special and we are not important in the eyes of the world. What many of us are, however, is deceived, because we think our value lies in our talents, money and accomplishments. Don't get me wrong: we have value—it is just not where we have placed it. Our value resides in the One who created us in His Own Image. We are special because He has created us to be higher than any other creature because we are the only creature created in His likeness.[60] He is special, and when we accept Him, we become special for eternity. Our value rests on the shoulders of the Son who was willing to die to give us life.[61]

We all have some written, imagined or vague mental blueprint by which we live life. These blueprints are drafted by our own past experiences, a goal we hope to obtain or through a deeply engrained mindset. Mindsets are primarily a set of attitudes passed down in families; other mindsets are learned in school or read in books. Humans tend to stick to what we know and believe. We engage in activities that make us feel comfortable. Sometimes when we are faced with a difficult situation, we often choose the path of least resistance. Some go against the grain, intentionally draw a new map and change everything to redefine themselves. Whatever map people choose to live their lives by, I would venture to say that many think their lives are on the right track. We feel good about what we believe, and we don't want anyone trying to persuade us otherwise.

Regardless of what we believe, a good reality check tells us that our lives are very short. Since we won't be on earth forever, it's time to examine ourselves to see if our lives are headed in the right direction. Why do we think our choices are the right ones? What do we hope to accomplish in our lives? When we take our last breath, what do we expect to happen? What is the purpose of our existence? These deep questions challenge us, and some might say they cannot be answered with any degree of certainty. We could surely agree that various views exist describing what will happen at the end of our earthly lives. Some believe

---

[60] Genesis 1:27
[61] John 3:16

we will die so something else can live. Others believe God will not allow anyone to go to Hell. Still others think that nothing happens—we will simply cease to exist. My challenge today is that we better know why we believe what we believe. We need to have no doubt in our mind that we are right. Our eternal destiny is riding on this choice, which is too big to leave to chance.

With so many views of what happens when we die being projected in society today, how can we possibly know which one is true? Many, who subscribe to relativism, say truth is what we believe it to be. Our truths are certainly exhibited in our lives. We live by what we believe truth to be.

But, what if there were a way to know Truth without a shadow of a doubt? What if we could have complete peace and reassurance in knowing the truth? What if there was no guesswork, no worrying about the outcome and no switching gears every time we changed our minds? Would we take that road? Would we grab it and run with all that is in us to bring about a brighter tomorrow? We have access to God's Word, which tells us what the truth is and has been.[62] Here's what happened: God decided what the truth would be. He then blessed us with His Holy Word, so we could have help creating or redrawing the blueprint of our lives. The Bible shows us the character of God, including His likes and His dislikes. It also tells us what to expect as He invites us to develop a relationship with Him.

God's Word sheds light on the truth of what has taken place before we were born, to keep us from walking in darkness during our lifetime. However sometimes we act like we think we know more than God or we want to be our own god. If we don't believe what God says, we are implying that He is a liar.[63] The source of God's Word is God. If we don't trust the Bible, then we don't trust God. The Bible contains all the proof that we need to follow God and live a fulfilled life. We will not be able to appear before a Holy God one day and say we didn't know about what He tells us in His Word.

It takes faith to believe in anything we have not seen ourselves. It seems, however, that many will believe many historical accounts more than they trust the accuracy of the Bible. Sometimes we hear something we think is important or interesting, and we share that information with others even if we don't actually know if it is true. So, why are we as

---

[62] 2 Timothy 3:16; John 1:1
[63] 1 John 5:9-10

humans prone not to believe the truth in the Bible? Many times it is because we don't like what it says or we don't trust the source.

We have a choice to make. We can believe God's Word or dismiss it. What we decide will affect our future. Not just a future here on Earth, but an everlasting future. We can chose to believe God and ask Him to help us change. We can humble ourselves and react to the truth that God reveals. God is merciful, but His anger is kindled by our disobedience.[64] If we disobey Him over and over again like the Israelites did, God's judgment will come as it did many times in the Old Testament. The question is: Will we receive His judgment by continuing in disobedience or will we escape it by obeying Him?

We need to be grounded in reality as we walk on borrowed land scheduled for destruction. We need to be diligent as we live with conflict and strive in vain for treasures we can't take with us. We need to face the facts that we may be willingly neglecting our relationship with the Almighty and jeopardizing our spiritual health and eternity to obtain an illusion of peace and ownership in a world where we are nothing more than a vapor.[65]

We have a loving Father who does not lie.[66] He said He has gone to prepare a place for us and that He is coming again to take us home. Heaven exists and is prepared for those who accept Jesus.[67] Hell is real and God doesn't want anyone to go there.[68] God's Apron of Truth will help us to live with confidence that our beliefs are grounded in more than theory and guesswork. God's Apron of Truth will help us know where we go when we die. His Truth protects us from other false after death theories—all of which originate from the Enemy.

---

[64] 2 Chronicles 30:7-8
[65] James 4:14
[66] Numbers 23:19
[67] John 14:1–6
[68] 2 Peter 3:9

Tying God's Apron Strings Around Your Heart

If you were to die tomorrow, would you be prepared? If you don't know, you may want to read what the Bible has to say about Heaven (Revelation Chapters 21 and 22)and Hell (Revelation 20:10;21:8; Luke16:22–31; and 2 Peter 2:4).There are only two options after we die.When you really understand the difference, I hope you will be motivated to make sure you know your eternal destination. Have you asked Jesus to save you so that you can spend eternity in Heaven with Him instead of in the pit of fire known as Hell? Settle this matter today. Then ask God to transform you so that you become more eternally minded for the rest of your life here on earth. Then you will be well prepared for the life to come.

Chapter 18
Forgiveness

"When you are in distress, and all these things come upon you in the latter days, when you turn to the LORD your God and obey His voice (for the LORD your God is a merciful God), He will not forsake you nor destroy you, nor forget the covenant of your fathers which He swore to them."
Deuteronomy 4:30-31, NKJV

I can hear the slow, mundane and melodious repeating of an all too familiar phrase of incantations as I approach the gathering at Topheth in the Valley of Hinnom. We are here to offer tribute to the god Molech by sacrificing our children. I methodically make my way through the mesmerized crowd. We are held captive as if by some ancient force gripping our souls. I feel it pushing me onward until I am at last standing at the base of a stone sculpture. The massive statue towers over me. Horns on either side of its head and flared nostrils send tremors of fear throughout my body. Its affixed and lusty arms demand the sacrificial, incomprehensible tribute of giving the lives of children. Heat exudes the smell of burning timber and surrounds the granite formation with a darkened cloud of intoxicating smoke billowing from within. The heat is so intense it causes the structure to glow like coals from the mere magnitude of the blaze. Fire reflects throughout the darkness leaving no one unaware of the sorcery intended this night.

I have been told that I am one of the lucky ones chosen from so many to sacrifice my most precious of gifts, my newborn child. You see, under this belief system, if we do not give what is most precious, our prayers will be hindered. This sacrifice will ensure that our prayers are heard and that the pagan gods are appeased. We are in dire need of answered prayer. Let's hope the gods hear us and are pleased with the tribute.

I am still weak from the travails of labor, my body shaking and my emotions are screaming in my head beyond my control. I hand my son to the priest. My heart aches, but out of fear for what may happen, I dare not show it. To reveal my grief would bring disapproval and judgment from the gods. I look to the stars, the constellations that I worship, but no comfort comes as my child is placed into the arms of death. I can almost hear the singe of delicate skin as it touches the hot stone. As the drums begin pounding louder to muffle the cries of the innocent, I can smell the undesirable aroma of burnt flesh as the fire desecrates the guiltless one's fragile frame. The gathering accelerates their mantra as the sacrifice burst into flames and is all but consumed. Dancing and chanting, cutting large gashes in their skin, the worshippers plead asking for blessings. They lift their hands as they beg and chant louder to be sure their prayers are heard. The ceremony lingers long into the night as the fire and the god's rage subsides.

All my hopes of what might have been are thrust into oblivion as I can feel a sickness rising up from within me. I tried not to love him, this child of mine. But, I do. Before he was born I could feel his movement within me growing and developing. I have given birth to him but he is no longer mine. He will not grow to be a man; he will never know love. He will never feel the evening breeze on his face or taste the sweetness of life. I chose to kill him—this naive one. I chose to end his life to appease the gods. I wearily return home and weep. Come morning, I wear a smile on my face though I am dying inside. I stay busy and everyone with their worries barely takes notice. I sought refuge but there is none. I am broken. The weight of the world is on my shoulders and I hold on so tight engulfed by fear that tells me if I let anything go, my entire life will collapse before me. The priests cast their spells and call upon their gods; but relief does not come. I live in a silent hell hidden from those who would condemn me for choosing this path. My course is set. I have no way out. If the gods are not appeased, our request will be denied. Our blessings in every way will be hindered. The life of others depends on the sacrifices given.

Life for some was much like this description of those living in the Kingdom of Judah shortly before King Josiah would take the throne. The Israelites had fallen into many practices where they offered themselves and their children as sacrifices in some way. God had adamantly commanded them not to get involved in the pagan religions that were rampant in the surrounding countries. But, they would not listen. It is hard for me to understand why a group of people, especially those who knew God as they had, could go as far as sacrificing their children to a false god, a god who is dead and has no power.

Even though this may seem farfetched, we are not much different today. We sacrifice our children to the gods of career, knowledge and selfishness. I know I was guilty of this sacrifice as my life was focused on striving for the earthly treasures of a nice house with new furniture, the latest car, stylish clothes, vacations and plenty of nice gifts for Christmas or birthdays. I would not give myself permission to relax until everything else was done. Instead of building an important relationship with my daughter, I was too busy trying to take care of all the things I owned and I was preoccupied striving to buy more things that I wanted or thought I had to have.

God graciously showed me how futile this quest for material goods was. The life I wanted was the life I had, but I couldn't enjoy it in the present because there was so much work to sustain the lifestyle for the future. God eventually showed me the moments of laughter that I missed because of my stressful to-do list. I had forgotten to pause and relish in once-in-a-lifetime moments like teaching my child to ride a bike or helping her bake her first batch of cookies. I praise God that He revealed my errant ways to me, and I am thankful that I now have another chance with my younger children to pause and enjoy those precious moments.

Although many women sacrifice their precious time with their living children like I did with my oldest child, at least those children get a change to live. Millions of other children are sacrificed each year to the god of abortion. Women have a number of reasons for making this choice. Like the lady who sacrificed her child in Josiah's era, I am sure every woman thinks it is the best choice or else she would not choose it. Many times fear is a large motivator. The lady in our story was afraid of what the gods would do if she didn't sacrifice her child. She then had to grieve in silence to appease the gods and make everyone else think everything was okay. Maybe she also had to keep convincing herself it was the right choice or she couldn't live with it. Either way, she was deceiving no one but herself. Her god, no matter how strongly she believed in it was nothing more than a pile of rock unable to deliver anything she asked. Her sacrifice was in vain. I am afraid some may feel that way today. A decision was made and now they have to grieve silently.

The tears God must shed at the mere influx of his beautiful creations being destroyed so thoughtlessly. Why is our life more valuable than those sacrificed? Oh, the thought of what might have been. A life snuffed out before it even had a chance to thrive. We are murdering future teachers and leaders of our nation. What kind of future are we planning? God will not allow us to pave our way on the exploitation of children not even unborn ones. God didn't like human sacrifice then and

His opinion hasn't changed. He is merciful, though. His kindness leads us to repentance, and He guides us as He enables us to change.

The requirements of the false gods in the Old Testament were cruel. They did not value life. This distortion of moral value is why God warned the Israelites about falling into such practices. God is not cruel. In fact, He gave His Son as the sacrifice so that we may have life.[69] He doesn't just offer us any life, but he offers us life abundantly. All that He requires of us, He also helps us with. He never leaves us to suffer alone. He is so loving and forgiving that even the sacrifice of a child to any god can be reconciled because of the blood of the One True God.

He offers His Apron to us, which is His shield against worldly thinking, which leads us to destructive choices or ungodly sacrifices without understanding their true consequences. His Apron is wide and strong and no one can penetrate it. His Apron of forgiveness through His Son Jesus can end our useless suffering if we will let it. Rediscover His forgiveness. Rediscover the power in His Shield, His Apron. Otherwise, we leave ourselves at the mercy of the god of this world, Satan. The Devil distorts the truth and keeps us captive in our guilt, shame and false security that comes when we have sinned and served the wrong gods.

Tying God's Apron Strings Around Your Heart

Do you feel guilty about your previous or current choices in life? Do you think God won't forgive you? Well, you couldn't be more wrong. Confess that large burden to Him and lay your guilt down at His feet. He is a loving Father. He will heal your brokenness if you will come to Him with a humble heart and a desire for a renewed relationship with Him. Don't you think it is about time you stopped pretending that everything is okay when it really isn't? God is patiently waiting to deliver you. Don't keep Him waiting, and don't keep hurting yourself any longer. He's already paid the price for your forgiveness. Let it go and receive His peace.

[69] John 3:16

Chapter 19
An Invitation

"Come to Me, all you who labor and are heavy laden, and I will give you rest. Take My yoke upon you and learn from Me, for I am gentle and lowly in heart, and you will find rest for your souls. For My yoke is easy and My burden is light."
Matthew 11:28–30, NKJV

Placed before us in a square white box. It is about the size of our dinner plate. Rough brown twine binds the box and makes it difficult to open. I search but can find nothing to cut the ropes so that I may see what's inside. A gentleman approaches and hands me a sword. He says it is the only thing that will free the box and allow me to access the box's contents. The twine is easily broken with this most unique sword, which he describes as "The Word of God."

With much anticipation, I open what I expect to be a wonderful present. But, I am unable to see its worth until much later. Below the lid, folded neatly in a square, is a linen napkin. The strings of the package fall as I retrieve the interior from the container allowing me to see inside. It is an apron.

Written in crimson on a bed of purity are the words: The Lord Jesus Christ. Upon further examination, I notice a small note in the box. It reads as follows:

Attention: For best results wear daily, wash often and keep the strings tied to transform your world.

Another note at the bottom of that page states:

Warning: Misuse and failure to follow instructions will lead to a host of unwelcome situations including—but not limited to—blindness, starvation, apathy and discontentment.

The gentleman who had handed me the sword lovingly said, "Put on the Apron,[70] the shield that protects you from the dingy chains that you

---

[70] Romans 13:12–14

have allowed to crowd out God. These chains have kept you in a box like prison of sin. You no longer have to live confined in suffocating circumstances. If you don't open this new box, or if you keep its lid closed tight and bound by sin, the life-giving contents inside—the Apron, otherwise known as Jesus the Savior—can't work through you. You will be rejecting His invitation and hampering His power from creating abundant life in you. Will you choose to accept His offer and access His Power freely so that He can be active in your life? Will you live for Him? Will you keep the strings of His Apron tied and will you flee from any temptation that tries to drag you down?"

Each day, as we walk in the world, we are giving others a taste of Jesus. Based on your life, would you say others know that God is good? Or, have you allowed a bad taste to linger in another's mouth because you say you wear Jesus, but somewhere along the way you have laid Him down? Have you kept going, not noticing that you have put Him aside like all the other projects that seemed exciting for a season, but now have lost your interest?

Jesus is motivated by what motivates His Father while Satan is motivated by death and suffering. When the truth is removed, all that is left is lies from Satan, the enemy. Don't fall prey to his schemes. Trust what God says today. Rediscover God's loving protection—the Apron— offered to us through the gift of His Son Jesus Christ. Rediscover the Truth and live like you have never lived before. Live with peace beyond your understanding; exude the quiet confidence that says God will never lie. But, you won't know that peace and confidence if you don't seek Him through the study of the Bible, time spent in prayer and a healthy dose of love for God's church. Neither you or any Christian can bear this world and its lies in isolation. If you have been rebelling from living God's way and have refused to be a part of a community, I encourage you to find a church home. If you have felt defeated, I urge you to stop being a downtrodden, discouraged Christian who rarely exudes the joy of the Lord, rarely reads the Truth and rarely takes time to pray. We are weak because we are not putting on God's Armor, and putting on the Armor starts with His Apron, Jesus Christ. We fall prey to the lies of Satan because we leave ourselves unprotected, with our apron strings dangling.

God's Apron is enough. It is multifaceted and free for the taking. But, we can't just grab it and go. God is not a convenience store; He is a lifestyle guru. We don't have to understand it all to accept it, but we do have to believe it and to keep His Word tied around us. We also have to trust Him as the ultimate Source. There is no other Source as trustworthy as He is. It is about time we tied the strings more tightly so that we no longer allow them to dangle on our Apron. With urgency in our actions, it is about time to get fired up. With God's help, it's time to stomp out the sin in our lives because Jesus is coming soon. I'm game. Won't you join me? What a ride it will be! Think of the stories we will be able to tell our children and grandchildren about God's protection and deliverance! He is a mighty King. May we serve Him well!

Tying God's Apron Strings Around Your Heart

A Final Exhortation: I hope you know how God delights in providing His Apron for you. I pray you have seen that tying the strings are a daily or even a moment-by-moment choice you need to make to seek Him in His Word and through prayer. I hope you have seen that you need others, in the faith, to help ensure your Apron strings stay tied. But, most of all, my greatest desire is for you to know that you have been called and equipped to play a part designed for you as He prepares us for His ultimate feast in Heaven. In the meantime, I hope you will find daily times of spiritual nourishment, enriching fulfillment and a deep soulful satisfaction from your preparatory meals with Him as your Teacher and your Ultimate Head Chef.

About the Author

Tammy Lovell Stone is a homeschool mom, preacher's wife, teacher and worship leader. She was a contributing author for Selah Press' *360 degrees of Grief: Reflections of Hope* and is involved in the next Selah Press Anthology to be published at a later date.

Tammy's next project, *Surge of Grace,* scheduled for release in early 2017, tells the true story of her journey of hope and healing from an unequally yoked marriage filled with selfishness and sometimes even misery to the God honoring, fulfilling and joyful marriage she has today.

Tammy is passionate about music and women's ministry. She enjoys gardening and spectacular sunsets viewed with her family from their 115-year- old homestead.

Tammy has been married for 29 years to her high school sweetheart, Kenny. Their children Ashton, Charley, Gabe, and grandchildren Britt and Boone reside in a small rural community outside of Nashville, Tennessee.

Tammy can be reached on Facebook or through her website, tammylovellstone.com. You may also check out her blog at rediscovertheapron.com

References

Jane Eyre. Universal, 2011. Film.

Ranier, Thom S. *Autopsy of a Deceased Church: 12 Ways to Keep Yours Alive.*"
B & H Publishing Group. May 1, 2014

Spafford, Horatio G. "It is Well with My Soul." Circa 1873

45849549R00062

Made in the USA
Charleston, SC
28 August 2015